Getting Started in

CURRENCY TRADING

The *Getting Started In* Series

Getting Started in

CURRENCY TRADING

Winning in Today's Hottest Marketplace

Michael D. Archer
Jim L. Bickford

WILEY

John Wiley & Sons, Inc.

For general information about our other products and services, please contact our Customer Care Department within the United States at 800-762-2974, outside the United States at 317-572-3993 or fax 317-572-4002.

Wiley also publishes its books in a variety of electronic formats. Some content that appears in print may not be available in electronic books. For more information about Wiley products, visit our web site at www.wiley.com.

ISBN-10 0-471-71303-1
ISBN-13 978-0-471-71303-6

Printed in the United States of America

10 9 8 7 6 5 4 3 2

Contents

PART 1

THEN AND NOW

Chapter 1

Chapter 2

PART 4

THE BUSINESS OF TRADING

Chapter 11

Acknowledgments

We would like to thank our personal friends Susan L. Cress and Gregory R. Morris for their meticulous assistance in design layout, organization, and editing. It is not surprising to find out that both have become avid small-cap FOREX traders since their involvement in editing this book.

Introduction

About This Book

This book is intended to introduce the novice investor to the exciting, complex, and sometimes profitable realm of trading world currencies on the foreign exchange markets (FOREX). It also serves as a reference guide for stocks and futures traders who wish to branch out into new securities opportunities. Our primary focus is on the rapidly expanding and evolving online trading marketplace for spot currencies.

From the very beginning we must emphasize that currency trading may not be to everyone's disposition. The neophyte investor must be keenly aware of all the risks involved and should never trade on funds he or she deems necessary for survival. If you have some experience with leveraged markets such as futures or options, you owe yourself a look at FOREX. Those who have never traded will find it the "purest" of all speculative adventures.

How This Book Is Organized

There are six main parts to this book:

1. Part 1—Then and Now

   Getting Started; History of Currency Trading; Currency Futures and the IMM

   We open the book with a questions-and-answer overview of the currency market in which we hope to dispel any myths the reader may have. We then proceed to a brief history and the current regulations surrounding the currencies market.

2. Part 2—What Every Trader Must Know

   FOREX Terms; Selecting a FOREX Broker; Opening an Online Trading Account; Mechanics of FOREX Trading; The Calculating Trader

Every lucrative industry has its own gamut of highly specialized terms, and currency trading is no exception. You must thoroughly comprehend these terms before attempting to initiate any trades. With a little familiarization, the jargon of currency trading will become second nature.

We will assist the new trader in selecting a reputable online currency dealer and explain the steps involved in opening a trading account. The actual step-by-step processes of initiating and liquidating a live market order are examined in detail with a lengthy explanation of each order type.

Currency trading requires some minimal record keeping. The novice investor will be pleased to know that the mathematics of trading and calculating profit or loss involves nothing more than simple, four-function arithmetic—addition, subtraction, multiplication and division—and that we have kept division examples to a minimum.

This section must be understood before the reader proceeds to the later sections.

3. Part 3—How to Beat the Market (Maybe)

Fundamental Analysis; Technical Analysis

Once the trader understands the mechanics of trading, he or she must develop a trading strategy. In Part 3, we assist the trader in formulating his own personalized trading schemes and tactics. Historically, there have been two major schools of thought in this endeavor: fundamental analysis and technical analysis. We explore the advantages and disadvantages of both schools in the chapters in this section.

4. Part 4—The Business of Trading

Money Management and Psychology; Trading Tactics; What to Do If Things Go Wrong; Record Keeping.

In this section, we expose the trader to the psychology of trading and the stresses that may accompany same. We place much emphasis on money management and psychology—two key topics that are vital to success but are often neglected in the search for the holy grail of trading methods.

5. Part 5—Advanced Topics

A single chapter covers Rollovers, Hedging, Options Trading, Arbitrage, Adding Complexity, and Pros and Cons of Arbitrage.

This section is optional for the novice trader though investors with some trading experience will find it informative.

6. Appendices

Our appendices section is very much a ready reference of FOREX-specific information.

We attempted to make *Getting Started in Currency Trading* an all-in-one introduction as well as a handy computer-side reference guide. Only you, the reader, may judge the level of our success therein.

Disclaimer

Neither the publisher nor the authors are liable for any financial losses incurred while trading currencies.

Part 1

Then and Now

1

Getting Started

What Is FOREX?

Foreign exchange is the simultaneous buying of one currency and selling of another. Currencies are traded through a broker or dealer and are executed in currency pairs; for example, the Euro dollar and the US dollar (EUR/USD) or the British pound and the Japanese yen (GBP/JPY).

The Foreign Exchange Market (FOREX) is the largest financial market in the world, with a volume of over $1.95 trillion daily. This is more than three times the total amount of the stocks and futures markets combined.

Unlike other financial markets, the FOREX spot market has neither a physical location nor a central exchange. It operates through an electronic network of banks, corporations, and individuals trading one currency for another. The lack of a physical exchange enables the FOREX market to operate on a 24-hour basis, spanning from one time zone to another across the major financial centers. This fact—that there is no centralized exchange—is important to keep in mind as it permeates all aspects of the FOREX experience.

What Is a Spot Market?

A spot market is any market that deals in the current price of a financial instrument. Futures markets, such as the Chicago Board of Trade, offer commodity contracts whose delivery date may span several months into the future.

TABLE 1.1	Major FOREX Currencies	
Symbol	*Country*	*Currency*
USD	United States	dollar
EUR	Euro members	Euro
JPY	Japan	yen
GBP	Great Britain	pound
CHF	Switzerland	franc
CAD	Canada	dollar
AUD	Australia	dollar

Settlement of FOREX spot transactions usually occurs within two business days. There are also futures and forwards in FOREX, but the overwhelming majority of traders use the spot market. We will discuss the opportunities to trade FOREX futures on the International Monetary Market.

Which Currencies Are Traded?

Any currency backed by an existing nation can be traded at the larger brokers. The trading volume of the major currencies (along with their symbols) is given in descending order: the U.S. dollar (USD), the Euro dollar (EUR), the Japanese yen (JPY), the British pound sterling (GBP), the Swiss franc (CHF), the Canadian dollar (CAD), and the Australian dollar (AUD). All other currencies are referred to as minors.

FOREX currency symbols are always three letters, where the first two letters identify the name of the country and the third letter identifies the name of that country's currency. (The "CH" in the Swiss franc acronym stands for Confederation Helvetica). See Table 1.1.

Who Trades on the Foreign Exchange?

There are two main groups that trade currencies. About five percent of daily volume is from companies and governments that buy or sell products and services in a foreign country and must subsequently convert profits made in foreign currencies into their own domestic currency in the course of doing business. This is primarily hedging activity. The other 95 percent consists of investors trading for profit, or speculation. Speculators range from large banks trading 10,000,000 million currency units or more and the home-based operator trading perhaps 10,000 units or less.

Today, importers and exporters, international portfolio managers, multinational corporations, speculators, day traders, long-term holders, and hedge funds all use the FOREX market to pay for goods and services, to transact in financial assets, or to reduce the risk of currency movements by hedging their exposure in other markets.

A producer of Widgets in the United Kingdom is intrinsically long the British pound (GBP). If they sign a long-term sales contract with a company in the United States, they may wish to buy some quantity of the USD and sell an equal quantity of the GBP to hedge their margins from a fall in the GBP.

The speculator trades to make a profit by purchasing one currency and simultaneously selling another. The hedger trades to protect his or her margin on an international sale (for example) from adverse currency fluctuations. The hedger has an intrinsic interest in one side of the market or the other. The speculator does not.

How Are Currency Prices Determined?

Currency prices are affected by a variety of economic and political conditions, but probably the most important are interest rates, international trade, inflation, and political stability. Sometimes governments actually participate in the foreign exchange market to influence the value of their currencies. They do this either by flooding the market with their domestic currency in an attempt to lower the price or, conversely, buying in order to raise the price. This is known as central bank intervention. Any of these factors, as well as large market orders, can cause high volatility in currency prices. However, the size and volume of the FOREX market make it impossible for any one entity to drive the market for any length of time.

Why Trade Foreign Currencies?

In today's marketplace, the dollar constantly fluctuates against the other currencies of the world. Several factors, such as the decline of global equity markets and declining world interest rates, have forced investors to pursue new opportunities. The global increase in trade and foreign investments has led to many national economies becoming interconnected with one another. This interconnection, and the resulting fluctuations in exchange rates, has created a huge international market: FOREX. For many investors, this has created exciting opportunities and new profit potentials. The FOREX market offers unmatched potential for profitable trading in any market condition or any stage of the business cycle. These factors equate to the following advantages:

- **No commissions.** No clearing fees, no exchange fees, no government fees, no brokerage fees.

- **No middlemen.** Spot currency trading does away with the middlemen and allows clients to interact directly with the market maker responsible for the pricing on a particular currency pair.

- **No fixed lot size.** In the futures markets, lot or contract sizes are determined by the exchanges. A standard-sized contract for silver futures is 5000 ounces. Even a "mini-contract" of silver, 1000 ounces, represents a value of approximately $6,000.00. In spot FOREX, *you* determine the lot size appropriate for your grubstake. This allows traders to effectively participate with accounts of well under $1,000.00.

- **Low transaction cost.** The retail transaction cost (the bid/ask spread) is typically less than 0.1 percent under normal market conditions. At larger dealers, the spread could be as low as 0.07 percent. This will be described in detail later.

- **High liquidity.** With an average trading volume of over $1.95 trillion per day, FOREX is the most liquid market in the world. It means that a trader can enter or exit the market at will in almost any market condition.

- **Almost instantaneous transactions.** This is a very advantageous by-product of high liquidity.

- **Low margin, high leverage.** These factors increase the potential for higher profits (and losses) and are discussed later.

- **A 24-hour market.** A trader may take advantage of all profitable market conditions at any time. There is no waiting for the opening bell.

- **Online access.** The big boom in FOREX came with the advent of online (Internet) trading platforms.

- **Not related to the stock market.** A trader in the FOREX market involves selling or buying one currency against another. Thus, there is no correlation between the foreign currency market and the stock market. A bull market or a bear market for a currency is defined in terms of the outlook for its relative value against other currencies. If the outlook is positive, we have a bull market in which a trader profits by buying the currency against other currencies. Conversely, if the outlook is pessimistic, we have a bull market for other currencies and traders take profits by selling the currency against other currencies. In either case, there is always a good market trading opportunity for a trader.

- **Interbank market.** The backbone of the FOREX market consists of a global network of dealers. They are mainly major commercial banks that communicate and trade with one another and with their clients through electronic networks and by telephone. There are no organized exchanges to serve as a central location to facilitate transactions the way the New York Stock Exchange serves the equity markets. The FOREX market operates in a manner similar to that of the NASDAQ market in the United States; thus it is also referred to as an over-the-counter (OTC) market.

- **No one can corner the market.** The FOREX market is so vast and has so many participants that no single entity, not even a central bank, can control the market price for an extended period of time. Even interventions by mighty central banks are becoming increasingly ineffectual and short-lived. Thus central banks are becoming less and less inclined to intervene to manipulate market prices. (You may remember the attempt to corner the silver futures market in the late 1970s. Such disruptive excess is not possible in the FOREX markets.)

- **No insider trading.** Because of the FOREX market's size and non-centralized nature, there is virtually no chance for ill effects caused by insider trading. Fraud possibilities, at least against the system as a whole, are significantly less than in any other financial instruments.

- **Limited regulation.** There is but limited governmental influence via regulation in the FOREX markets, primarily because there is no centralized location or exchange. Of course, this is a sword that may cut both ways, but the authors believe—with a hardy caveat emptor—that less regulation is, on balance, an advantage. Nevertheless, most countries do have some regulatory say and more seems on the way. Regardless, fraud is always fraud wherever it is found and subject to criminal penalties in all countries.

Traditionally, investors' only means of gaining access to the foreign exchange market was through banks that transacted large amounts of currencies for commercial and investment purposes. Trading volume has increased rapidly over time, especially after exchange rates were allowed to float freely in 1971.

What Tools Do I Need to
Trade Currencies?

A computer with reliable (and preferably fast) Internet access and the information in this book are all that is needed to begin trading currencies.

What Does It Cost to Trade Currencies?

An online currency trading account (a "mini-account") may be opened for as little as $100. Do not laugh—mini-accounts are a good way to get your feet wet without taking a bath. Unlike futures, where the size of a contract is set by the exchanges, in FOREX you select how much of any particular currency you wish to buy or sell. Thus, a $3,000.00 grubstake is not unreasonable as long as the trader engages in appropriately sized trades. FOREX mini-accounts also do not suffer the illiquidity of many futures mini-contracts, as everyone feeds from the same currency "pool."

FOREX Versus Stocks

Historically, the securities markets have been considered, at least by the majority of the public, as an investment vehicle. In the last ten years, securities have taken on a more speculative nature. This was perhaps due to the downfall of the overall stock market as many security issues experienced extreme volatility because of the "irrational exuberance" displayed in the marketplace. The implied return associated with an investment was no longer true. Many traders engaged in the day trader rush of the late 1990s only to discover that from a leverage standpoint it took quite a bit of capital to day trade, and the return—while potentially higher than long-term investing—was not exponential, to say the least.

After the onset of the day trader rush, many traders moved into the futures stock index markets where they found they could better leverage their capital and not have their capital tied up when it could be earning interest or making money somewhere else. Like the futures markets, spot currency trading is an excellent vehicle for the pattern day trader that desires to leverage his or her current capital to trade. Spot currency trading provides more options and greater volatility while at the same time stronger trends than are currently available in stock futures indexes. Former securities day traders have an excellent home in the FOREX market.

There are approximately 4,000 stocks listed on the New York Stock Exchange. Another 2,800 are listed on the NASDAQ. Which one will you trade? Trading just the seven major USD currency pairs instead of 7,800 stocks simplifies matters significantly for the FOREX trader. Fewer decisions, fewer headaches.

FOREX Versus Futures

The futures contract is precisely that—a legally binding agreement to deliver or accept delivery of a specified grade and quantity of a given commodity in a distant month. FOREX, however, is a spot (cash) market in which trades rarely exceed two days. Many FOREX brokers allow their investors to "roll over" open trades after two days. There exist FOREX futures or forward contracts, but almost all activity is in the spot market facilitated by rollovers.

In addition to the advantages listed, FOREX trades are almost always executed at the time and price asked by the speculator. There are numerous horror stories about futures traders being locked into an open position even after placing the liquidation order. The high liquidity of the foreign exchange market (roughly three times the trading volume of all the futures markets combined) ensures the prompt execution of all orders (entry, exit, limit, etc.) at the desired price and time.

The caveat here is something called a requote which we will discuss in a later chapter.

The Commodity Futures Trading Commission (CFTC) authorizes futures exchanges to place daily limits on contracts that significantly hamper the ability to enter and exit the market at a selected price and time. No such limits exist in the FOREX market.

Stock and futures traders are used to thinking in terms of the U.S. dollar versus something else, such as the price of a stock or the price of wheat. This is like comparing apples to oranges. In currency trading, however, it's always a comparison of one currency to another currency—someone's apples to someone else's apples. This paradigm shift can take a little getting used to, but we will give you plenty of examples to help smooth the transition.

We must reiterate: There is always some risk in speculation regardless of which financial instruments are traded and where they are traded, regulated or unregulated.

Summary

- FOREX means "Foreign Exchange."
- The FOREX market is a $1.95 trillion-a-day financial market, dwarfing everything else including stocks and futures.
- There is no centralized exchange or clearing house for currency trading.
- The FOREX market is less regulated than other financial markets.
- The top four traded currencies are: the U.S. dollar (USD), the European dollar (EUR), the Japanese yen (JPY), and the British pound (GBP).
- Access to the FOREX markets via the Internet has resulted in a great deal of interest by small traders previously locked out of this enormous marketplace.

2

History of
Currency Trading

This material may not seem very relevant to trading currencies today, but a little perspective never hurts.

Ancient Times

Foreign exchange dealing may be traced back to the early stages of history, possibly beginning with the introduction of coinage by the ancient Egyptians, and the use of paper notes by the Babylonians. Certainly by biblical times, the Middle East saw a rudimentary international monetary system when the Roman gold coin *aureus* gained worldwide acceptance followed by the silver *denarius*, both a common stock among money changers of the period.

By the Middle Ages, foreign exchange became a function of international banking with the growth in the use of bills of exchange by the merchant princes and international debt papers by the budding European powers in the course of their underwriting the period's wars.

The Gold Standard, 1816–1933

The gold standard was a fixed commodity standard: participating countries fixed a physical weight of gold for the currency in circulation, making it directly redeemable in the form of the precious metal. In 1816 for instance, the pound sterling was defined as 123.27 grains of gold, which was on its way to becoming the foremost reserve currency and was at the time the principal component of the international capital market. This led to the expression "as good as gold" when applied to Sterling—the Bank of England at the time gained stability and prestige as the premier monetary authority.

Of the major currencies, the U.S. dollar adopted the gold standard late in 1879 and became the standard-bearer, replacing the British pound when Britain and other European countries came off the system with the outbreak of World War I in 1914. Eventually, though, the worsening international depression led even the dollar off the gold standard by 1933; this marked the period of collapse in international trade and financial flows prior to World War II.

The "Fed"

As an investor, it is essential to acquire a basic knowledge of the Federal Reserve System (the Fed). The Federal Reserve was created by the U.S. Congress in 1913. Before that, the U.S. government lacked any formal organization for studying and implementing monetary policy. Consequently, markets were often unstable and the public had very little faith in the banking system. The Fed is an independent entity, but is subject to oversight from Congress. This means that decisions do not have to be ratified by the president or anyone else in the government, but Congress periodically reviews the Fed's activities.

The Fed is headed by a government agency in Washington known as the Board of Governors of the Federal Reserve. The Board of Governors consists of seven presidential appointees, who each serve 14-year terms. All members must be confirmed by the Senate, and they can be reappointed. The board is led by a chairman and a vice chairman, each appointed by the president and approved by the Senate for four year terms. The current chair is Alan Greenspan, who has been chairman since 1987. His latest term expires in 2006.

There are 12 regional Federal Reserve Banks located in major cities around the country that operate under the supervision of the Board of Governors. Reserve Banks act as the operating arm of the central bank and do most of the work of the Fed. The banks generate their own income from four main sources:

1. Services provided to banks
2. Interest earned on government securities
3. Income from foreign currency held
4. Interest on loans to depository institutions

The income generated from these activities is used to finance day-to-day operations, including information gathering and economic research. Any excess income is funneled back into the U.S. Treasury.

The system also includes the Federal Open Market Committee, better known as the FOMC. This is the policy-creating branch of the Federal Reserve. Traditionally the chair of the board is also selected as the chair of the FOMC. The voting members of the FOMC are the seven members of the Board of Governors, the president of the Federal Reserve Bank of New York, and presidents of four other Reserve Banks who serve on a one-year rotating basis. All Reserve Bank presidents participate in FOMC policy discussions whether or not they are voting members. The FOMC makes the important decisions on interest rates and other monetary policies. This is the reason they get most of the attention in the media.

The primary responsibility of the Fed is "to promote sustainable growth, high levels of employment, stability of prices to help preserve the purchasing power of the dollar, and moderate long-term interest rates."

In other words, the Fed's job is to foster a sound banking system and a healthy economy. To accomplish its mission the Fed serves as the banker's bank, the government's bank, the regulator of financial institutions, and as the nation's money manager.

The Fed also issues all coin and paper currency. The U.S. Treasury actually produces the cash, but the Fed Banks then distributes it to financial institutions. It is also the Fed's responsibility to check bills for wear and tear, taking damaged currency out of circulation.

The Federal Reserve Board (FRB) has regulation and supervision responsibilities over banks. This includes monitoring banks that are members of the system, international banking facilities in the United States, foreign activities of member banks, and the U.S. activities of foreign-owned banks. The Fed also helps to ensure that banks act in the public's interest by helping in the development of federal laws governing consumer credit. Examples are the Truth in Lending Act, the Equal Credit Opportunity Act, the Home Mortgage Disclosure Act, and the Truth in Savings Act. In short, the FED is the policeman for banking activities within the United States and abroad.

The FRB also sets margin requirements for investors. This limits the amount of money you can borrow to purchase securities. Currently, the requirement is set at 50 percent, meaning that with $500 you have the opportunity to purchase up to $1000 worth of securities.

Securities and Exchange Commission, 1933–1934

When the stock market crashed in October 1929, countless investors lost their fortunes. Banks also lost great sums of money in the Crash because they had invested heavily in the markets. When people feared their banks might not be able to pay back the money that depositors had in their accounts, a "run" on the banking system caused many bank failures.

With the Crash and ensuing depression, public confidence in the markets plummeted. There was a consensus that for the economy to recover, the public's faith in the capital markets needed to be restored. Congress held hearings to identify the problems and search for solutions.

Based on the findings in these hearings, Congress passed the Securities Act of 1933 and the Securities Exchange Act of 1934. These laws were designed to restore investor confidence in capital markets by providing more structure and government oversight. The main purposes of these laws can be reduced to two common-sense notions:

1. Companies that publicly offer securities for investment dollars must tell the public the truth about their businesses, the securities they are selling, and the risks involved in investing.

2. People who sell and trade securities—brokers, dealers, and exchanges— must treat investors fairly and honestly, putting investors' interests first.

The Bretton Woods System, 1944–1973

The post-World War II period saw Great Britain's economy in ruins, its infrastructure having been bombed. The country's confidence with its currency was at a low. By contrast, the United States, thanks to its physical isolation, was left relatively unscathed by the war. Its industrial might was ready to be turned to civilian purposes. This then has led to the dollar's rise to prominence, becoming the reserve currency of choice and staple to the international financial markets.

Bretton Woods came about in July 1944 when 45 countries attended, at the behest of the United States, a conference to formulate a new international financial framework. This framework was designed to ensure prosperity in the post-war period and prevent the recurrence of the 1930s global depression. Named after a resort hotel in New Hampshire, the Bretton Woods system formalized the role of the U.S. dollar as the new global reserve currency, with its value fixed into gold. The United States assumed the responsibility of ensuring convertibility while other currencies were pegged to the dollar.

Among the key features of the new framework were:

• Fixed but adjustable exchange rates
• The International Monetary Fund
• The World Bank

The End of Bretton Woods and Floating Exchange Rates

After close to three decades of running the international financial system, Bretton Woods finally went the way of history due to growing structural imbalances among the economies, leading to mounting volatility and speculation in a one-year period from June 1972 to June 1973. At the time the United Kingdom, facing deficit problems, initially floated the sterling. Then it was devaluated further in February of 1973 losing 11 percent of its value along with the Swiss franc and the Japanese yen. This eventually led to the European Economic Community floating their currencies as well.

At the core of Bretton Woods' problems were deteriorating confidence in the dollars' ability to maintain full convertibility and the unwillingness of surplus countries to revalue for its adverse impact in external trade. Despite a last-ditch effort by the Group of Ten finance ministers through the Smithsonian Agreement in December 1971, the international financial system from 1973 onwards saw market-driven floating exchange rates taking hold. Several times efforts for reestablishing controlled systems were undertaken with varying levels of success. The most well known of these was Europe's Exchange Rate Mechanism of the 1990s which eventually led to the European Monetary Union.

International Monetary Market

In December 1972, the International Monetary Market (IMM) was incorporated as a division of the Chicago Mercantile Exchange (CME) that specialized in currency futures, interest-rate futures, and stock index futures, as well as futures options.

Commodity Futures Trading Commission

In 1974 Congress created the Commodity Futures Trading Commission (CFTC) as an independent agency with the mandate to regulate commodity futures and options markets in the United States. The agency is chartered to protect market participants against manipulation, abusive trade practices, and fraud.

Through effective oversight and regulation, the CFTC enables the markets to better serve their important functions in the nation's economy, providing a mechanism for price discovery and a means of offsetting price risk. The CFTC also seeks to protect customers by requiring three things: that registrants disclose market risks and past performance information to prospective customers, that customer funds be kept in accounts separate from those maintained by the firm for its own use, and that customer accounts be adjusted to reflect the current market value at the close of trading each day.

National Futures Association

The National Futures Association (NFA), created in 1982, is a quasi-private, self-regulatory agency established by the CFTC and participants in the futures markets. The NFA sets standards for the registration of professionals with the authority to impose limited fines for breach of conduct. NFA is the premier independent provider of efficient and innovative regulatory programs that safeguard the integrity of the derivatives markets and directs the regulatory actions of the CFTC into the marketplace.

Commodity Futures Modernization Act of 2000

The Commodity Futures Trading Commission (CFTC) proposed rules relating to trading facilities to implement the Commodity Futures Modernization Act of 2000 (CFMA). On December 15, 2000, Congress passed, and on December 21, 2000, the president signed into law, the CFMA, which substantially altered the Commodity Exchange Act. The CFMA amended the law to establish three categories of markets: designated contract markets, derivative transaction execution facilities, and markets exempt from CFTC regulation. The three categories match the degree of regulation to the varying nature of the products and the nature of the participant having access to the market.

Beginning in the 1980s, cross-border capital movements accelerated with the advent of computers and technology, extending market continuum through Asian, European, and American time zones. Transactions in foreign exchange rocketed from about $70 billion a day in the 1980s to more than $1.85 trillion a day two decades later.

Keep in mind that the Modernization Act pertains mostly to futures and forwards, *not* cash/spot markets. However, the CFTC seems to be gaining more and more momentum for some form of FOREX cash regulation within the boundaries of the United States.

The NFA stipulates that members cannot transact with non-members. So, for example, if your FOREX broker/dealer is an NFA member, he or she must consent to being regulated and is not allowed to do business with non-NFA money managers. We would not accept a broker simply because he or she is an NFA member; nor would we condemn one who is not a member. It is still a "buyer beware" marketplace.

Currency trading remains much less regulated than either the stock or futures markets. This means the prospective trader must be especially *knowledge-*

able, alert, and *realistic.* As the market has opened up to the small speculator, it has also opened up the market for less-than-scrupulous companies and individuals. Remember: If it's too good to be true—it probably is! The non-centralized nature of FOREX makes the level of regulation seen in the futures market unlikely to be attained.

Check in on the CFTC and NFA Web sites from time to time for actions against broker/dealers and for updates on any pending regulation that might affect U.S.–based FOREX traders.

Refer to the Appendix entitled "Regulatory Agencies and Central Banks" for information on obtaining the complete text of the Modernization Act.

Regulation in Other Countries

Nearly every major country around the globe has created a government agency responsible for overseeing the conduct of trading securities and protecting investors from fraudulent dealers and scam artists. In the United Kingdom, this agency is called the Financial Services Authority (FSA) and in Australia it is called the Australian Securities and Investment Commission (ASIC). Refer to the Appendix entitled "Regulatory Agencies and Central Banks" for further details.

The Arrival of the Euro

On January 1, 2002, the Euro became the official currency of twelve European nations that agreed to remove their previous currencies from circulation prior to February 28, 2002. See Table 2.1.

TABLE 2.1 European Monetary Union	
Austria	schilling
Belgium	franc
Finland	markka
France	franc
Germany	mark
Greece	drachma
Ireland	punt
Italy	lira
Luxembourg	franc
Netherlands	guilder
Portugal	escudo
Spain	peseta

The Euro was considered an immediate success and is now the second most frequently traded currency in FOREX markets. More details on the Euro can be found in the Appendix of this book.

Table 2.2 depicts the major events in FOREX history and regulation.

TABLE 2.2   Timeline of Foreign Exchange

1913—U.S. Congress creates the Federal Reserve System.

1933—Congress passes the Securities Act of 1933 to counter the effects of the Great Crash of 1929.

1934—The Securities Exchange Act of 1934 creates the beginnings of the Securities and Exchange Commission.

1936—The Commodity Exchange Act is enacted in direct response to manipulating grain and futures markets.

1944—The Bretton Woods Accord is established to help stabilize the global economy after World War II.

1971—The Smithsonian Agreement is established to allow for a greater fluctuation band for currencies.

1972—The European Joint Float is established as the European community tries to move away from their dependency on the U.S. dollar.

1972—The International Monetary Market is created as a division of the Chicago Mercantile Exchange.

1973—The Smithsonian Agreement and European Joint Float fail, signifying the official switch to a free-floating system.

1974—Congress creates the Commodity Futures Trading Commission to regulate the futures and options markets.

1978—The European Monetary System is introduced to again try to gain independence from the U.S. dollar.

1978—The Free-floating system is officially mandated by the International Monetary Fund.

1993—The European Monetary System fails to make way for a worldwide, free-floating system.

1994—Online currency trading makes its debut.

2000—Commodity Modernization Act establishes new regulations for securities derivatives, including currencies in futures or forwards form.

2002—The Euro becomes the official currency of twelve European nations on January 1.

Summary

- Until the late 1960s the currency markets were extremely stable and very much a closed club. Things were about to change rapidly!

- Currency trading is probably the world's *second*-oldest profession!

- The Euro, introduced in 2002, is the official currency of twelve European countries: Austria, Belgium, Finland, France, Germany, Greece, Ireland, Italy, Luxembourg, the Netherlands, Portugal, and Spain.

- Key dates and events—1973, 1978, 1994, 2002

- The trend is towards more regulation of cash/spot currency markets. Traders should watch the actions of the Commodity Futures Trading Commission (CFTC) and its quasi-independent administration arm, the National Futures Associations (NFA). Do not take regulation as an excuse for not doing your own homework!

Chapter

3

Currency Futures and the IMM

Futures Contracts

A futures contract is an agreement between two parties: a short position, the party who agrees to deliver a commodity, and a long position, the party who agrees to receive a commodity. For example, a grain farmer would be the holder of the short position (agreeing to sell the grain) while the bakery would be the holder of the long (agreeing to buy the grain).

In a futures contract, everything is precisely specified: the quantity and quality of the underlying commodity, the specific price per unit, and the date and method of delivery. The price of a futures contract is represented by the agreed-upon price of the underlying commodity or financial instrument that will be delivered in the future. For example, in the grain scenario, the price of the contract might be 5,000 bushels of grain at a price of four dollars per bushel and the delivery date may be the third Wednesday in September of the current year.

Currency Futures

The FOREX market is essentially a cash or spot market in which over 90 percent of the trades are liquidated within 48 hours. Currency trades held longer than this are normally routed through an authorized commodity futures exchange such as the International Monetary Market. IMM was founded in 1972 and is a division of the Chicago Mercantile Exchange (CME) that specializes in currency futures, interest-rate futures, and stock index futures, as well as options on futures. Clearing houses (the futures exchange) and introducing brokers are subject to more stringent regulations from the SEC, CFTC, and NFA agencies than the FOREX spot market (see *www.cme.com* for more details).

It should also be noted that FOREX traders are charged only a transaction cost per trade, which is simply the difference between the current bid and ask prices. Currency futures traders are charged a round-turn commission that varies from broker house to broker house. In addition, margin requirements for futures contracts are usually slightly higher than the requirements for the FOREX spot market.

Contract Specifications

Table 3.1 is a list of currencies traded through IMM at the Chicago Mercantile Exchange and their contract specifications.

Size represents one contract requirement though some brokers offer mini-contracts, usually one-tenth the size of the standard contract. Months identify the month of contract delivery. The tick symbols H, M, U, Z are abbreviations for March, June, September, and December respectively. Hours indicate the

		TABLE 3.1	**Currency Contract Specifications**		
Commodity	Contract Size		Months	Hours	Minimum Fluctuation
Australian dollar	100,000	AUD	H, M, U, Z	7:20–14:00	0.0001 AUD = $10.00
British pound	62,500	GBP	H, M, U, Z	7:20–14:15	0.0002 GBP = $12.50
Canadian dollar	100,000	CAD	H, M, U, Z	7:20–14:00	0.0001 CAD = $10.00
Eurocurrency	62,500	EUR	H, M, U, Z	7:20–14:15	0.0001 EUR = $ 6.25
Japanese yen	12,500,000	JPY	H, M, U, Z	7:00–14:00	0.0001 JPY = $12.50
Mexican peso	500,000	MXN	All months	7:00–14:00	0.0025 MXN = $12.50
New Zealand dollar	100,000	NZD	H, M, U, Z	7:00–14:00	0.0001 NZD = $10.00
Russian ruble	2,500,00	RUR	H, M, U, Z	7:20–14:00	0.0001 RUR = $25.00
South African rand	5,000,000	ZAR	All months	7:20–14:00	0.0025 ZAR = $12.50
Swiss franc	62,500	CHF	H, M, U, Z	7:20–14:15	0.0001 CHF = $12.50

local trading hours in Chicago. The minimum fluctuation represents the smallest monetary unit that is registered as one pip in price movement at the exchange and is usually one-ten thousandth of the base currency.

Currencies Trading Volume

Table 3.2 summarizes the trading activity of selected futures contracts in currencies, precious metals, and some financial instruments. The volume and open interest readings are *not* trade signals. They are intended only to provide a brief synopsis of each market's liquidity and volatility based on the average of 30 trading days.

TABLE 3.2	Futures Volume and Open Interest			
Market	*Sym*	*Exch*	*Vol*	*OI*
S&P 500 e-mini	ES	CME	489.1	377.9
Nasdaq 100 e-mini	NQ	CME	237.0	158.4
Eurodollar	ED	CME	93.9	772.5
S&P 500	SP	CME	59.3	531.4
Eurocurrency	EC	CME	49.5	112.9
Mini Dow	YM	CBOT	48.1	30.2
10-year T-note	TY	CBOT	43.1	676.4
Gold	GC	NYMEX	33.7	163.0
5-year T-note	FV	CBOT	29.6	582.8
30-year T-bond	US	CBOT	25.9	324.1
Japanese yen	JY	CME	18.6	132.1
Canadian dollar	CD	CME	18.0	64.2
Nasdaq 100	ND	CME	13.3	65.4
British pound	BP	CME	12.2	58.3
Silver	SI	NYMEX	10.0	84.2
Swiss franc	SF	CME	9.3	45.6
Mexican peso	ME	CME	8.8	30.5
Dow Jones	DJ	CBOT	8.7	29.5
Aussie dollar	AD	CME	7.8	55.7
2-year T-note	TU	CME	7.0	108.6
Copper	HG	NYMEX	4.2	32.8

Legend: *Sym:* Ticker symbol, *Exch:* Futures exchange on which contract is traded, *Vol:* 30-day average daily volume, in thousands, *OI:* Open interest, in thousands.

Source: Active Trader Magazine, January 16, 2004 *(www.activetradermag.com).*

TABLE 3.3 U.S. Dollar Index	
Currency	Weight %
Eurocurrency	57.6
Japanese yen	13.6
British pound	11.9
Canadian dollar	9.1
Swedish krona	4.2
Swiss franc	3.6

U.S. Dollar Index

The U.S. Dollar Index (ticker symbol = DX) is an openly traded futures con-tract offered by the New York Board of Trade. It is computed using a trade-weighted geometric average of six currencies. See Table 3.3.

IMM currency futures traders monitor the U.S. Dollar Index to gauge the dollar's overall performance in world currency markets. If the Dollar Index is trending lower, then it is very likely that a major currency that is a component of the Dollar Index is trading higher. When a currency trader takes a quick glance at the price of the U.S. Dollar Index, it gives the trader a good feel for what is going on in the FOREX market worldwide.

For traders who are interested in more details on commodity futures, we recommend Todd Lofton's paperbound book, *Getting Started in Futures* (2001: John Wiley & Sons, Inc.).

Part

What Every Trader Must Know

FOREX Terms

As in any worthwhile endeavor, each industry tends to create its own unique lingo. The FOREX market is no different. You, the novice trader, must thoroughly comprehend certain terms before making your first trade.

Currency Pairs

Every FOREX trade involves the simultaneous buying of one currency and the selling of another currency. These two currencies are always referred to as the currency pair in a trade.

Major and Minor Currencies

The seven most frequently traded currencies (USD, EUR, JPY, GBP, CHF, CAD, and AUD) are called the major currencies. All other currencies are referred to as minor currencies. The most frequently traded minors are the New Zealand dollar (NZD), the South African rand (ZAR), and the Singapore dollar (SGD). After that, the frequency is difficult to ascertain because of perpetually changing trade agreements in the international arena.

Cross Currency

A cross currency is any pair in which neither currency is the U.S. dollar. These pairs may exhibit erratic price behavior since the trader has, in effect, initiated two USD trades. For example, initiating a long (buy) EUR/GBP trade is equivalent to buying a EUR/USD currency pair and selling a GBP/USD. Cross currency pairs frequently carry a higher transaction cost. The three most frequently traded cross rates are EUR/JPY, GBP/EUR, and GBP/JPY.

Base Currency

The base currency is the first currency in any currency pair. It shows how much the base currency is worth as measured against the second currency. For example, if the USD/CHF rate equals 1.6215, then one USD is worth CHF 1.6215. In the FOREX markets, the U.S. dollar is normally considered the "base" currency for quotes, meaning that quotes are expressed as a unit of $1 USD per the other currency quoted in the pair. The primary exceptions to this rule are the British pound, the Euro, and the Australian dollar.

Quote Currency

The quote currency is the second currency in any currency pair. This is frequently called the pip currency and any unrealized profit or loss is expressed in this currency.

Pips

A pip is the smallest unit of price for any foreign currency. Nearly all currency pairs consist of five significant digits and most pairs have the decimal point immediately after the first digit, that is, EUR/USD equals 1.2812. In this instance, a single pip equals the smallest change in the fourth decimal place, that is, 0.0001. Therefore, if the quote currency in any pair is USD, then one pip always equals $\frac{1}{100}$ of a cent.

One notable exception is the USD/JPY pair where a pip equals $ 0.01 (one U.S. dollar equals approximately 107.19 Japanese yen). Pips are sometimes called points.

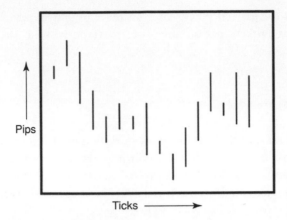

Pips

Ticks ⟶

FIGURE 4.1   Pip-tick relationship.

Ticks

Just as a pip is the smallest price movement (the *y*-axis), a tick is the smallest interval of time (the *x*-axis) that occurs between two trades. When trading the most active currency pairs (such as EUR/USD or USD/JPY) during peak trading periods, multiple ticks may (and will) occur within the span of one second. When trading a low-activity minor cross pair (such as the Mexican peso and the Singapore dollar), a tick may only occur once every two or three hours.

Ticks, therefore, do not occur at uniform intervals of time. Fortunately, most historical data vendors will "group" sequences of streaming data and calculate the open, high, low, and close over regular time intervals (1-minute, 5-minute, 30-minute, 1-hour, daily, and so forth.). See Figure 4.1.

Margin

When an investor opens a new margin account with a FOREX broker, he or she must deposit a minimum amount of monies with that broker. This minimum varies from broker to broker and can be as low as $100.00 to as high as $100,000.00.

Each time the trader executes a new trade, a certain percentage of the account balance in the margin account will be earmarked as the initial margin requirement for the new trade based upon the underlying currency pair, its current price, and the number of units traded, (called a lot). The lot size always refers to the base currency. An even lot is usually a quantity of 100,000 units, but most brokers permit investors to trade in odd lots (fractions of 100,000 units).

Leverage

Leverage is the ratio of the amount used in a transaction to the required security deposit (margin). It is the ability to control large dollar amounts of a security with a comparatively small amount of capital. Leveraging varies dramatically with different brokers, ranging from 10:1 to 100:1. Leverage is frequently referred to as gearing. The formula for calculating leverage is:

$$\text{Leverage} = 100/\text{Margin Percent}$$

Bid Price

The bid is the price at which the market is prepared to buy a specific currency pair in the FOREX market. At this price, the trader can sell the base currency. It is shown on the left side of the quotation. For example, in the quote USD/CHF 1.4527/32, the bid price is 1.4527; meaning you can sell one U.S. dollar for 1.4527 Swiss francs.

Ask Price

The ask is the price at which the market is prepared to sell a specific currency pair in the FOREX market. At this price, the trader can buy the base currency. It is shown on the right side of the quotation. For example, in the quote USD/CHF 1.4527/32, the ask price is 1.4532; meaning you can buy one U.S. dollar for 1.4532 Swiss francs. The ask price is also called the offer price.

Bid/Ask Spread

The spread is the difference between the bid and ask price. The "big figure quote" is the dealer expression referring to the first few digits of an exchange rate. These digits are often omitted in dealer quotes. For example, a USD/JPY rate might be 117.30/117.35, but would be quoted verbally without the first three digits as "30/35."

TABLE 4.1	Examples of Quote Convention
EUR/USD	1.2604/07
GBP/USD	1.5089/94
CHF/JPY	84.40/45

Quote Convention

Exchange rates in the FOREX market are expressed using the following format:

Base Currency / Quote Currency   Bid/Ask

Examples can be found in Table 4.1.

Normally only the final two digits of the bid price are shown. If the ask price is more than 100 pips above the bid price, then three digits will be displayed to the right of the slash mark (that is, EUR/CZK 32.5420/780). This only occurs when the quote currency is a very weak monetary unit.

Transaction Cost

The critical characteristic of the bid/ask spread is that it is also the transaction cost for a round-turn trade. Round-turn means both a buy (or sell) trade and an offsetting sell (or buy) trade of the same size in the same currency pair. In the case of the EUR/USD rate in Table 4.1, the transaction cost is three pips. The formula for calculating the transaction cost is:

Transaction Cost = Ask Price − Bid Price

Rollover

Rollover is the process whereby the settlement of an open trade is rolled forward to another value date. The cost of this process is based on the interest rate differential of the two currencies.

Putting It All Together

Trading currencies on margin lets you increase your buying power. If you have $2,000 cash in a margin account that allows 100:1 leverage, you could purchase up to $200,000 worth of currency because you only have to post one percent of the purchase price as collateral. Another way of saying this is that you have $200,000 in buying power.

With more buying power, you can increase your total return on investment with less cash outlay. To be sure, trading on margin magnifies your profits *and* your losses.

A detailed description on how to calculate profit and loss of leveraged trades occurs in Chapter 8: The Calculating Trader.

The Trader's Nemesis

All traders fear the dreaded margin call. This occurs when the broker notifies the trader that his or her margin deposits have fallen below the required minimum level because an open position has moved against the trader.

Trading on margin can be a profitable investment strategy, but it is important that you take the time to understand the risks. You should make sure you fully understand how your margin account works. Be sure to read the margin agreement between you and your clearing firm. Talk to your account representative if you have any questions.

The positions in your account could be partially or totally liquidated should the available margin in your account fall below a predetermined threshold. You may not receive a margin call before your positions are liquidated.

Margin calls can be effectively avoided by monitoring your account balance on a very regular basis and by utilizing stop-loss orders (discussed later) on every open position to limit risk. For ease of use, most online trading platforms automatically calculate the profit and loss of a trader's open positions.

Margin Calls

Nearly all FOREX brokers monitor your account balance continuously. If your balance falls below four percent of the open margin requirement, they will issue the first margin call warning, usually by an online pop-up message on the screen and/or an email notification. If your account balance drops below three percent of the margin requirement for your open positions, they will issue a second margin warning. At two percent, they will liquidate all your open trades and notify you of your current account balance. These percentages may vary from broker to broker.

Selecting a FOREX Broker

Caveat Emptor

Before selecting an Internet or online FOREX broker, the new investor should closely examine the services that each candidate dealer offers and the policies that it mandates.

Since the passage of the Commodity Futures Modernization Act of 2000, the CFTC's Division of Enforcement has filed 41 FOREX cases in eleven states: 14 in Florida; 10 in California; 6 in New York; 3 in Georgia; 2 in Utah; and one each in Michigan, North Carolina, Ohio, Oregon, Texas, and Washington. The defendants in these actions defrauded approximately 3,400 retail investors. These scam artists advertised continually on radio and television. They promised unrealistic profits on very modest investments. They offered bid/ask spreads in excess of 30 pips while charging a $200 commission per trade.

The novice trader must be aware of Off-Exchange Currency Dealers (derogatorily called "bucket shops"). When selecting a prospective FOREX broker, find out with which regulatory agencies each dealer is registered, if any. The FOREX market is billed as an "unregulated" market, and essentially it is. Regulation is typically reactive, occurring only after the damage has been done.

There are numerous safe and reputable FOREX brokers from which to choose; consider your specific needs and likes/dislikes before making a selection.

Broker Services

Online Trading Platform

Nearly all FOREX brokers allow their clients to conduct trading over the Internet in a clear and comprehensible fashion. The backbone of any trading platform is, of course, the order entry process.

Examine the dealer's screen layout: It should include a bar chart of the currency pair being monitored, an account summary showing the trader's current account balance with realized and unrealized profit and loss, margin available, and any margin locked in active positions. A list of currently held positions should also be displayed on the same Web page, or at least be readily accessible.

Most trading platforms are either in Windows or Java format; some dealers offer both versions. A few trading platforms are appearing with Flash.

Some investors may prefer to use voice brokers to execute their trades as in the pre-Internet era. This service must be specifically mentioned in the broker's list of services since telephone trading is a waning method of trading in the new millennium.

While the authors much prefer the online format, we highly recommend finding a dealer who offers a voice backup—the Internet can do strange things, often at the wrong time.

Charting Packages

Some dealers are now offering integrated charting and technical analysis packages with their dealing platform, or partnerships with charting services. These are definitely worth exploring if the charts or technical tools offered are of value to your method of trading. The level of integration with the dealing platform also varies and is worth understanding carefully.

Here are a few to consider (there are more):

- *www.gaincapital.com*
- *www.gftforex.com*
- *www.refcofx.com*

Some of the charting services offering robust FOREX are:

- *www.tradestation.com*
- *www.esignal.com*
- *www.aspenres.com*

We are told Trade Station will soon integrate with the dealing platform of *www.rjobrien.com*.

Paper Trading

Numerous dealers provide a "paper trading" service that allows the beginning trader to become acclimated to the real market and "test" a given trading strategy without risk. These brokers provide a free demo account in which the investor places orders in a real-time environment but no money exchanges hands. These trades exist only on paper and are not executed by the broker. After a week or two of paper trading, the new trader can then assess his or her potential for profit or loss in the "real" market and proceed accordingly.

Micro-Accounts

Some dealers offer very small "mini-accounts" for as little as $100, although we feel even a mini-account should have at least a $1000 balance. Micro-accounts are a great way to get started and test your basic trading expertise and acumen. Even trading with very small amounts is much more telling than paper trading. But the broker you use for a micro-account may not be the one you want to use for "real" trading.

Online Assistance

Though not a requisite, some brokers offer education services and training courses for the first-time trader. Also the trading platform should have a robust Help directory on its main menu Web page. Additionally, each candidate broker should list an email address for customer service queries.

News Services

Before beginning a new trading session, the experienced trader will normally peruse the news articles that his or her broker has posted to a news articles Web page. Though this service is not requisite, it is very informative and may affect the trader's choices for which currency pairs and which positions to take for that session.

Chat Rooms

Many dealers sponsor open chat rooms for their member clients that focus on currency trading. Many of the questions that a new trader has are frequently answered in chat rooms. Be cautious of unsolicited trade tips in these chat rooms and on the discussion boards—or from anywhere, for that matter.

Other Services

Other services are up to the whim of the individual trader, such as multilingual platforms, advanced charting, technical and fundamental analysis add-ins, and various accounting system options. It is also wise to see with which regulatory agencies the candidate broker is registered (CFTC, NFA, and so on). In addition, examining a broker's FAQ Web page will guide the new trader through the services and options available.

Broker Policies

Available Currency Pairs

The new trader should confirm that the prospective broker offers the seven major currencies (AUD, CAD, CHF, EUR, GBP, JPY, and USD). Certain cross currency pairs (a pair in which neither currency is USD) may not be available, since this entails extra risk.

Transaction Costs

As described earlier, transaction costs are calculated in terms of pips. The lower the number of pips required per trade by the broker, the greater the profit that the trader makes. Comparing pip spreads of a half dozen brokers or so will reveal different transaction costs. One arbitrary rule of thumb is that the bid/ask spread for EUR/USD (the most frequently traded currency pair) should never exceed three or four pips, and a two-pip transaction cost is highly preferable.

Margin Requirement

The lower the margin requirement (and hence the higher the leverage), the greater the potential for higher profits and losses. Margin percentages can vary from 1 percent to 10 percent.

Low margin requirements are great when your trades are good, but not so great when you are wrong. Be realistic about margins and remember that they swing both ways. In general, low margins are nice to have available, although you may not normally want to take full advantage of them.

Minimum Trading Size Requirement

The size of one lot may vary from broker to broker, spanning 1,000, 10,000, and 100,000 units. These brokers usually offer a mini-lot, which is one-tenth of a lot. Ideally, a broker offers fractional unit sizes (called odd lots) to allow the trader to select any unit size that he or she wants.

Rollover Charges

Rollover charges are determined by the difference between U.S. interest rates and the interest rates in the corresponding country. The greater the interest rate differential between the two currencies in the currency pair, the greater the rollover charge will be. For example, if the British pound has the greatest differential with the U.S. dollar, then the rollover charge for holding British pound positions would be the most expensive. Conversely, if the Swiss franc were to have the smallest interest rate differential to the U.S. dollar, then overnight charges for USD/CHF would be the least expensive of the currency pairs. The whole rollover mechanism is discussed in detail in Chapter 8, on advanced topics.

Margin Account Interest Rate

Most brokers pay interest on a trader's margin account. The interest rates normally fluctuate with the prevailing national rates. At least the equity in your margin account will be accruing interest if you decide to take an extended break from trading.

Trading Hours

Nearly all brokers align their hours of operation to coincide with the hours of operation of the global FOREX market: 5:00 PM EST Sunday through 4:00 PM EST Friday. Confirm this when selecting a dealer.

Other Policies

Be certain to scrutinize a prospective broker's "fine print" section to be fully aware of all the nuances that a specific broker may impose on a new trader.

There are several active forums and discussion groups on currency trading on the Internet. Spend a little time in these forums reviewing what others have experienced with certain brokers. Feel free to ask questions, too. Do not get addicted to the discussion groups and forums, however. Although they are a great way to occasionally find information and share information, they are, for the most part, a distraction to the serious trader. The authors check in with the top two or three boards about once a week for perhaps ten minutes each, maximum.

The premier board at this time is *www.moneytec.com,* but also worthy of mention is *www.global-view.com.* Both of these boards accept paid advertising. Check in with these forums while doing your initial due diligence, thereafter on a periodic basis. Again, do not become addicted to them.

Broker Selection Process

- No broker/dealer is perfect. Having no centralized exchange makes the selection process very important; the total number of distinct platforms is now well over 100!

- Start with at least three prospects so you may do comparables and perhaps negotiate if you are opening a larger account (typically over $25,000).

- Ask for references with whom you can speak on the telephone.

- Check the regulatory agencies in the country in which the broker resides if the broker/dealer is regulated.

- Go to the various FOREX discussion groups on the Internet. Look for information on that broker. Ask questions, too. But be careful—the person answering you may be the broker or one of the broker's "representatives."

- *Requoting.* This is the major complaint against online brokers. It occurs when the trading platform *does not* give you the quote you select on the screen, but something else, not as good—perhaps as much as 10 pips difference. You're not likely to find an online broker who doesn't requote occasionally, but beware brokers who requote often, especially when you are winning!

  Requoting is a very much discussed topic today in the FOREX community. Because there is no centralized exchange it is going to happen from time to time. When reviewing the requoting of a broker/dealer it is important to ask 1) *How often does it occur?* and 2) *When does it occur?* If requoting happens in fast-moving markets, it's probably the nature of the beast. If it happens whenever you have a big winning trade, beware.

- Review all of the broker's paperwork (typically downloadable from the broker's site). Compare it to others for wording, terms, and so on.

- Send a list of email questions to each of your initial prospects—this is to get answers and to test for responsiveness.

- Call the broker's telephone number to see if voice contact is reliable. The authors would not personally deal with a broker who does not offer a voice backup or customer service support line.

- Compare especially: account minimums, costs (pip spreads), the handling of account withdrawals (time period), and margin. Pips vary from currency pair to currency pair, the most popular having the lowest spread; two pips for the EUR/USD pair is not uncommon. Some dealers may charge a small "lot fee" that can add up quickly, so be sure to ask if a dealer has such a fee and what it is. Get hard copy printouts of everything.

Broker Selection Process *(continued)*
• Finally, you will want to spend some time with the broker's online Dealing or Trading Platform paper trade, and then trade a mini-account for 30 days. Most trading platforms are *not* bug-free—it's extremely complicated software and real-time delivery over the Internet is not a small task.
• Check the discussion boards for other traders' experiences.

Finding the right broker/dealer is a critical part of the process. It is not easy and requires some real work on your part. Do not pick the first one that looks good to you. Keep looking. Do not be necessarily put off by persistent sales representatives but be sure to shun high-pressure sales tactics.

Avoiding Fraudulent Operations

There are several levels of FOREX dealers with online access:

Bucket shops. These have essentially *no* connection to the real-world FOREX market. The identifying characteristic on most of these is that they heavily tout currency futures and options over spot FOREX.

Book makers. These are perfectly legitimate in some countries and fine if you want to simply place a "bet" on a currency. One Web site to explore is *www.deltaindex.com.*

Top on your list should be:
1. Does the broker have a good recommendation?
2. How did it score on the broker selection process?
3. Do you feel comfortable with the trading platform? Is it reliable?
4. Does the broker offer telephone *and* email means of communication and trade back-up?
5. Are costs in line with the market? Especially pip spreads and margins?
6. What are the requoting experiences of other traders?

Retail market makers (RMMs). These represent the vast majority of online dealers. There is a wide spectrum amongst them with respect to their organizational form and how much they actually connect *directly* to the FOREX market. One such dealer is actually a U.S.–domiciled bank: *www.cbfx.com.*

A few other RMMs are:

- *www.refcofx.com*
- *www.gftforex.com*
- *www.saxobank.com*
- *www.sbfx.net*
- *www.gaincapital.com*

Institutional market makers. These are very closely aligned with the FOREX interbank market, and are great if you have enough for their minimum account requirement. Two examples are *www.hotspot.com* and *www.fxall.com.*

Institutional FOREX. At the top of the heap is the Intranet-based trading system, EBS. This is actually a consortium of close to 200 banks and represents well over 50 percent of bank FOREX trading. You must be a bank to participate. For more, see *www.ebs.com.*

It is still critical that traders investigate the integrity of prospective brokers as well as their services, costs, and trading platforms. Some traders jump from one dealer to another in the blink of an eye. Don't do it; rather, investigate thoroughly beforehand.

6

Opening an Online Trading Account

O pening a new account with an Internet FOREX broker usually consists of four simple steps: selecting an account type, registration, account activation, and confirmation. Consider opening micro or mini-accounts with two or three broker/dealers and ultimately consolidating your money to the one that seems to work best for you. Take time making a decision you can live with: Don't be rushed and don't be afraid to ask lots and lots of questions! But once you decide on a dealer, try to stick with it unless you realize you've made a very big mistake.

Account Types

FOREX brokers offer individual and corporate accounts. There may also be different account types based on the size of the initial equities that a trader deposits with the broker. Read the fine print first.

Many brokers offer managed accounts in which the dealer makes all the decisions on which currency pairs to buy and sell and which trade sizes to transact. This is equivalent to depositing equities into some form of investment instrument (such as mutual funds) but with a higher risk factor. It also removes the intrigue and emotional aspect of trading your private account.

Make sure you are opening a FOREX *spot* account and not a FOREX forwards or futures account. Almost everyone uses the spot market, as it is easy to

TABLE 6.1   Account Registration Forms
Application form
Risk disclosure statement
Consent to conduct business electronically
Customer agreement
W-9 tax form

rollover your position should you wish to hold it for more than a single session of trading. Also, most of the fraud in the FOREX game has been seen in the forwards and futures arena.

Registration

The required paperwork to register a new account varies from broker to broker but always includes the items shown in Table 6.1.

These are usually provided in PDF (portable document format) format and can be printed using your Adobe Acrobat program. A free download of this great program is available at: *http://www.adobe.com/products/acrobat/ readstep2.html.*

Discuss any questions on the telephone whenever possible and get answers, clarifications, changes, and promises in writing.

Account Activation

The broker will email you the necessary steps to activate your new trading account after receipt of your initial deposit and the required application forms.

Identification Confirmation

Upon account activation, you will have to confirm your identification by email. You will be assigned a user name and password that you use each time you enter a trading session.

Before signing and returning the broker's application forms, be certain that you feel comfortable with the following broker policies since you are entering a binding contractual agreement:

- The broker's hours of operation.
- The bid/ask pip spread on major currency pairs.
- The amount of margin that the broker requires per trade.
- The minimum trading unit size.
- There are no hidden commission costs or other trading fees.
- The reliability of the trading platform.
- Charting and technical analysis services. These are either add-on or integrated into the trading platform.
- Requoting policy. Be sure to get this in writing.

Last, never send the broker money that you consider non-disposable. If you are too anxious about your money, you will not make good trading decisions. If this happens, trade down to a sleeping level.

Chapter

7

Mechanics of FOREX Trading

I n this chapter, we discuss the variety of orders that may be placed into the market. The basic rule of thumb, especially for novice traders, is to *keep it simple*. Make certain you know which types of orders your broker/dealer accepts and build your trading system accordingly. Conversely, if your trading system requires complex order methodologies (we hope it does not), be sure the broker you select can comfortably handle them.

Different broker/dealers accept (and do not accept) different types of orders. Once you have developed your trading plan you will be able to determine which types of orders are "must haves" for you.

Order Types

Basic Order Types

There are some basic order types that all brokers provide and some others that are more esoteric. The basic ones are:

- **Market orders.** A market order is an order to buy or sell at the current market price. Remember in currency trading, you are *buying* or *selling* one currency *against* another currency.

- **Limit orders.** A limit order is an order placed to buy or sell at a certain price. The order essentially contains two variables, price and duration.

The trader specifies the price at which he or she wishes to buy/sell a certain currency pair and also specifies the duration that the order should remain active.

- **Limit entry orders.** Limit entry orders are executed when the exchange rate touches (but does not break) a specific level. The client placing a limit entry order believes that after touching a specific level, the rate will bounce in the opposite direction of its previous momentum.

- **Stop-loss orders.** A stop-loss is a limit order linked to a specific position for the purpose of stopping the position from accruing additional losses. A stop-loss order placed on a buy position is a stop entry order to sell linked to that position. A stop-loss order remains in effect until the position is liquidated or the client cancels the stop-loss order.

- **Take profit orders.** A take profit order is a limit order linked to a specific position for the purpose of capturing accrued profits and liquidating the position. A take profit order remains in effect until the position is liquidated or the client cancels the take profit order.

Esoteric Order Types

The following more esoteric orders may not be available at all dealers and are usually just variations of other order types or involve a specified duration of time:

- **GTC (Good 'til canceled).** A GTC order remains active in the market until the trader decides to cancel it. The dealer will not cancel the order at any time, therefore it is the customer's responsibility to remember that he or she possesses the order.

- **GFD (Good for the day).** A GFD order remains active in the market until the end of the trading day. Because foreign exchange is an ongoing market, the end of day must be a set hour.

- **OCO (Order cancels other).** An OCO order is a mixture of two limit and/or stop-loss orders. Two orders with price and duration variables are placed above and below the current price. When one of the orders is executed the other order is canceled. Example: The price of EUR/USD is 0.9340. The trader wants to either buy 10,000 at 0.9395 over the resistance level in anticipation of a breakout or initiate a selling position if the price falls to 0.9300. The understanding is that if 0.9395 is reached, the trader will buy 10,000 and the 0.9300 order will be automatically canceled.

Always read your broker's documentation for specific order information and to see if any rollover fees will be applied if a position is held longer than one day. Keeping your ordering rules simple is the best strategy.

Most online broker/dealers are not among the small pool of institutional FOREX market makers. They can give instantaneous orders primarily because they are "throwing off" bulk orders to larger dealers—sometimes market makers. The bid-ask spread is not only part of their profit picture, but protects them against fluctuations in the market.

Once you decide which order types you need for trading (generally speaking, fewer is best), check out the brokers on your list to see which ones will best accommodate you.

Order Execution

Traders using an online trading platform click on the "buy" or "sell" button after having specified the underlying currency pair and the desired number of units to trade. The execution of the order is instantaneous. This means that the price seen at the exact time of the click will be given to the customer. See Figures 7.1 and 7.2.

Placing a market order by phone is quite similar but usually takes a few seconds more. The exact process is as shown in Table 7.1.

FIGURE 7.1 Market order request.

Limit Order		
ACTION	BUY ▼	
CURRENCY	EUR/USD ▼	
UNITS	10000	
QUOTE	1.2613	
DURATION	12 HOURS ▼	
☑ Stop Loss	1.2633	
☑ Take Profit	1.2583	
Submit	Cancel	

FIGURE 7.2   Limit order request.

Order Confirmation

Online traders receive a screen message indicating confirmation of an order within seconds after the trade has been executed, as shown in Figure 7.3.

Traders can also cancel any limit order that has not been executed at any time. Most brokers respond with a message similar to the one seen in Figure 7.4.

Voice traders usually receive a verbal confirmation within 5 to 15 seconds after placing the order.

TABLE 7.1   Order Sequence
1. A customer specifies the currency pair and the deal size to the dealer.
2. The dealer gives a two-way price (bid and ask price).
3. The customer takes one of the two prices (he or she may ask for a requote).
4. The dealer confirms the trade. Under normal market conditions, dealers usually respond to market orders in about 5 to 10 seconds at most. Assuming the customer deals immediately on the offered prices, the average phone deal can be made in 10 to 15 seconds.

FIGURE 7.3 Order confirmation message.

Transaction Exposure

All online trading platforms are obligated to inform the investor of his or her current status in the FOREX market. Most will display this critical information in a window similar to the one seen in Figure 7.5.

The abbreviation GTC in the Expiry (expiration date) column in Figure 7.5 stands for "Good 'Til Canceled."

FIGURE 7.4 Limit order cancellation.

Trades and Orders								
Open Trades								
Ticket	Position	Currency	Units	Stop Loss	Take Profit	Price	Market	Profit
1458 1246	Buy	EUR/USD	10000	1.2625	1.2675	1.2650	1.2658	+8 Pips
1458 1267	Sell	USD/JPY	5000	105.95	105.35	105.65	105.70	-5 Pips
Limit Orders								
Ticket	Position	Currency	Units	Stop Loss	Take Profit	Price	Market	Expiry
1458 1246	S/L	EUR/USD	10000	n/a	n/a	1.2625	1.2658	GTC
1458 1246	T/P	EUR/USD	10000	n/a	n/a	1.2675	1.2658	GTC
1458 1267	S/L	USD/JPY	5000	n/a	n/a	105.95	105.70	GTC
1458 1267	T/P	USD/JPY	5000	n/a	n/a	105.35	105.70	GTC

FIGURE 7.5   Transaction exposure.

Summary

The basic order types (market, stop loss, and take profit) are usually all that most traders ever need. Unless you are a veteran trader, do not design a system of trading requiring a large number of orders sandwiched in the market at all times—stick with the basic stuff first.

If you are using an online trading platform: *before submitting an order,* close your eyes for a moment, then check all aspects of your order before clicking "submit." The two most common errors here are selecting "buy" (the default) when "sell" was intended and entering an incorrect number of units.

Make certain you fully understand and are comfortable with your broker's order entry system before executing a trade. *Do not* make a trade with real money until you have an extremely high comfort level with the trading platform and order entry system.

Chapter

8

The Calculating Trader

Here is where the rubber meets the road. Take your time with this information, as it is necessary knowledge for all FOREX traders. We recommend that you do not even paper trade until you are completely comfortable with pip values and calculating profit and loss for any pairs or crosses you intend to trade.

Profit and Loss (P&L) for every open position is calculated in real-time on most brokers' trading platforms. The information in this chapter enables traders to track their own P&L tick by tick as the market fluctuates.

Leverage and Margin Percent

Some brokers describe their gearing in terms of a leverage ratio and others in terms of a margin percentage. The simple relationships between the two terms are:

Leverage = 100 / Margin Percent

Margin Percent = 100 / Leverage

Leverage is conventionally displayed as a ratio, such as 20:1 or 50:1. In the examples that follow which require leverage, we use only the number on the left side of the ratio—that is, 20 or 50—since the number on the right side is always 1.

Pip Values

A pip is the smallest price increment that any currency pair can move in either direction. In the FOREX markets, profits are calculated in terms of pips first, then dollars second. See Table 8.1.

Approximate USD values for a one-pip move per contract in the major currency pairs are shown in Table 8.2, per 100,000 units of the base currency.

On a typical day, actively traded currency pairs like EUR/USD and USD/JPY can fluctuate 100 pips or more. The above table is based upon a margin requirement of 100 percent (leverage = 1:1). To calculate actual profit (or loss) in leveraged positions, multiply the pip value per 100k times the leverage ratio (margin percentage divided by 100).

Note that the EUR/GBP cross rate pair in Table 8.2 uses multiplication with the USD spot price instead of division. This is because the USD is the quote (second) currency in the spot conversion pair.

TABLE 8.1 Single Pip Values	
USD = Quote Currency	
EUR/USD	.0001 USD
GBP/USD	.0001 USD
AUD/USD	.0001 USD
USD = Base Currency	
USD/JPY	.01 JPY
USD/CHF	.0001 CHF
USD/CAD	.0001 CAD
Non-USD Cross Rates	
EUR/JPY	.01 JPY
EUR/CHF	.0001 CHF
EUR/GBP	.0001 GBP
GBP/JPY	.01 JPY
GBP/CHF	.0001 CHF
CHF/JPY	.01 JPY

TABLE 8.2 Full Lot Pip Values	
Currencies	*1 Pip Value Per Full Lot (100,000 units)*
EUR/USD	EUR 100,000 × .0001 = USD 10.00
GBP/USD	GBP 100,000 × .0001 = USD 10.00
AUD/USD	AUD 100,000 × .0001 = USD 10.00
USD/JPY	USD 100,000 × .01 = JPY 1,000 / USDJPY spot (105.50) = USD 9.47
USD/CHF	USD 100,000 × .0001 = CHF 10.00 / USDCHF spot (1.2335) = USD 8.11
USD/CAD	USD 100,000 × .0001 = CAD 10.00 / USDCAD spot (1.3148) = USD 7.61
EUR/JPY	EUR 100,000 × .01 = JPY 1,000 / USDJPY spot (105.50) = USD 9.47
EUR/CHF	EUR 100,000 × .0001 = CHF 10.00 / USDCHF spot (1.2335) = USD 8.11
EUR/GBP	EUR 100,000 × .0001 = CHF 10.00 × GBPUSD spot (1.8890) = USD 5.2
GBP/JPY	GBP 100,000 × .01 = JPY 1,000 / USDJPY spot (105.50) = USD 9.47
GBP/CHF	GBP 100,000 × .0001 = CHF 10.00 / USDCHF spot (1.2335) = USD 8.11
CHF/JPY	CHF 100,000 × .01 = JPY 1,000 / USDJPY spot (105.50) = USD 9.47

Calculating Profit and Loss

Many FOREX trading platforms offer their clients a variety of online utilities that assist the investor in his or her trading calculations. The utility to compute the profit or loss on each trade should resemble what is shown in Figure 8.1.

Because all profits are expressed in U.S. dollars, a key factor in the calculation of profit and loss is the currency pair and whether the USD is the base currency or the quote currency, or if the currency pair is a non-USD cross rate. Therefore, we will present several examples involving all cases.

Remember that the first currency in a currency pair is called the base currency (determines the number of units traded) and the second is called the quote currency (determines the pip values of each price change).

Scenario 1

USD Is the Quote Currency (Profit)

Currency pair. Select the corresponding currency pair from the dropdown list. The default is the EUR/USD pair.

Position. Choose either "buy" or "sell." The default is "buy."

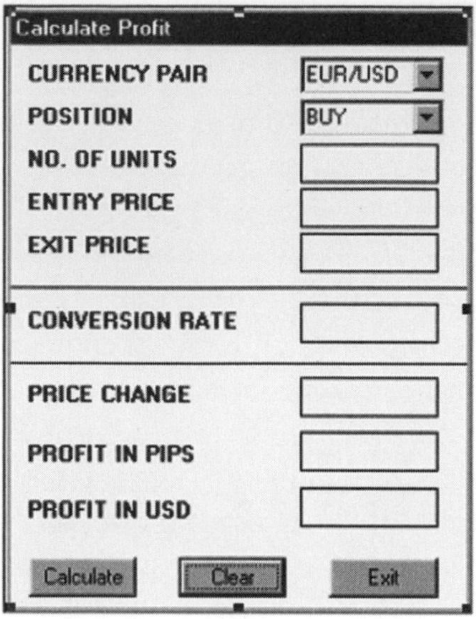

FIGURE 8.1   Online profit calculator.

Number of units. This is the individual number of units and *not* the number of lots or mini-lots. A full lot should be entered as "100000" and a mini-lot as "10000."

Entry price. This is the entry price regardless if the trade was a market order or a limit order. Include the decimal point.

Exit price. This is the liquidation price regardless if the trade was manually exited or a limit order was triggered.

Conversion rate. This entry is necessary to convert any profit or loss to U.S. dollars if the quote currency (the second one in the pair) is not USD. In this example, USD is the quote currency. Enter the single digit "1" since we already have conversion parity. Other possibilities are explained later.

Click the "Calculate" button as shown in Figure 8.2.

In this example we bought a mini-lot (10,000 units) of the EUR/USD pair at 1.2563 and sold at 1.2588, netting a clear profit of 25 pips (price change times pip factor, or $0.0025 \times 10,000$). The price change is simply:

$$\text{Price Change} = \text{Exit Price} - \text{Entry Price}$$

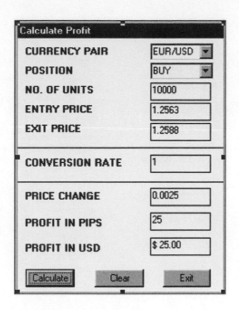

FIGURE 8.2 A 25-pip profit in EUR/USD.

The pip factor is the number of pips in the monetary unit of quote currency. There are 10,000 pips in one U.S. dollar and, conversely a single pip equals $0.0001. The pip factor is therefore 10,000.

$$\text{Profit in Pips} = \text{Price Change} \times \text{Pip Factor}$$

When the quote currency is the USD, profit or loss is calculated very simply as:

$$\text{Profit in USD} = \text{Price Change} \times \text{Units Traded}$$

In our scenario, this equates to:

$$\$\,25.00 = 0.0025 \times 10{,}000$$

Many of you have just exclaimed "Wow! That was painlessly simple. Show me one more!"

Scenario 2

USD Is the Quote Currency (Loss) For those of you who exclaimed nothing or are staring blankly at this page, we will do it again, this time with the GBP/USD currency pair. See Figure 8.3.

```
┌─────────────────────────────────────────────┐
│ Calculate Profit                              │
│                                               │
│   CURRENCY PAIR        │GBP/USD ▼│            │
│   POSITION             │SELL     ▼│           │
│   NO. OF UNITS         │30000    │            │
│   ENTRY PRICE          │1.8863   │            │
│   EXIT PRICE           │1.8883   │            │
│                                               │
│   CONVERSION RATE      │1        │            │
│                                               │
│   PRICE CHANGE         │-0.0020  │            │
│   PROFIT IN PIPS       │-20      │            │
│   PROFIT IN USD        │-$ 60.00 │            │
│                                               │
│  │Calculate│    Clear        Exit             │
└─────────────────────────────────────────────┘
```

FIGURE 8.3   A 20-pip loss in GBP/USD.

In this instance, we initiated a 30,000-unit short (sell) trade in the GBP/USD pair at 1.8863 and, sadly, it advanced against our hopes. We exited at 1.8883, losing 20 pips. Since the quote currency (the second currency) is USD, we know the conversion rate is 1. Thus using the profit formula

$$\text{Profit in USD} = \text{Price Change} \times \text{Units Traded}$$

we find that our profit is actually a loss:

$$-\$60.00 = -0.0020 \times 30000$$

If the above calculations are still causing some confusion, we recommend that you take a break, then reread Chapter 4, "FOREX Terms." As promised before, these calculations only require the four simple arithmetic functions: addition, subtraction, multiplication, and division. No exponents, logs, or trig functions. But this information must be completely clear before proceeding. Keep in mind that it is your money at stake.

Scenario 3

USD Is the Base Currency (Profit)   If the quote (second) currency is not the U.S. dollar, then profit or loss must be converted to U.S. dollars. For example, a

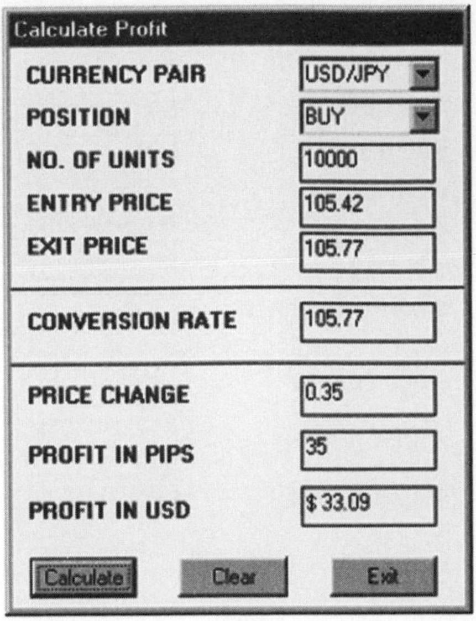

FIGURE 8.4 A 35-pip profit in USD/JPY.

35-pip profit in the USD/JPY pair means that the 35 pips are expressed in Japanese yen (see Figure 8.4). Therefore, one extra step is required to convert yen to dollars:

Conversion Rate. If USD is the base currency of the currency pair being calculated, then divide the profit or loss by the exit price. This simply converts the pip profit expressed as yens to a profit expressed as dollars.

Thus, when calculating currency pairs where the base (first) currency is the U.S. dollar, the profit formula must be adjusted as follows:

$$\text{Profit in USD} = \text{Price Change} \times \text{Units Traded} / \text{Exit Price}$$

or, specifically:

$$\$33.09 = 0.35 \times 10000 / 105.77$$

Obviously, all U.S. brokers perform this simple conversion to U.S. dollars before adding profits to your margin account.

Scenario 4

USD Is the Base Currency (Loss) This example is arithmetically identical to the previous example, except that a small loss was incurred. We purchased 5,000

```
┌─────────────────────────────────────────────┐
│ Calculate Profit                            │
│                                             │
│   CURRENCY PAIR        │USD/CAD ▼│          │
│   POSITION             │BUY     ▼│          │
│   NO. OF UNITS         │5000     │          │
│   ENTRY PRICE          │1.3152   │          │
│   EXIT PRICE           │1.3142   │          │
│                                             │
│   CONVERSION RATE      │1.3142   │          │
│                                             │
│   PRICE CHANGE         │-0.0010  │          │
│   PROFIT IN PIPS       │-10      │          │
│   PROFIT IN USD        │-$ 3.80  │          │
│                                             │
│   [ Calculate ]    Clear      Exit          │
└─────────────────────────────────────────────┘
```

FIGURE 8.5   A 10-pip loss in USD/CAD.

units of the USD/CAD pair at 1.3152 and set a stop-loss limit order at 1.3142, which, unfortunately, was triggered (see Figure 8.5).

Using the same adjusted profit formula as in the previous example,

$$\text{Profit in USD} = \text{Price Change} \times \text{Units Traded} / \text{Exit Price}$$

we find:

$$-\$3.80 = -0.0010 \times 5000 / 1.3142$$

Note: Always keep your losses small.

Scenario 5

Non-USD Cross Rates (USD/Quote)   Most experienced traders can mentally perform the arithmetic in the above examples. It just takes practice. However, we must now tackle cross rates, currency pairs where neither currency is the U.S. dollar. Obviously the profit in pips will be initially expressed in terms of the quote (second) currency of the cross rate pair. The solution is simple: Look up the current price of the currency pair containing USD and the quote currency of the cross rate pair, as shown in Figure 8.6.

The Conversion Rate entry of 105.32 in Figure 8.6 is actually the current price of the USD/JPY pair. The adjusted profit formula for this cross rate trade is:

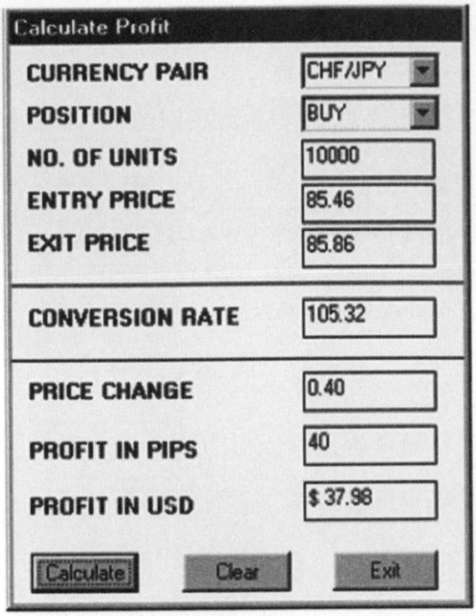

FIGURE 8.6   A 40-pip profit in CHF/JPY.

Profit in USD = Price Change × Units Traded / Conversion Rate

or

$$\$37.98 = 0.40 \times 10000 / 105.43$$

A pattern is developing here . . .

Scenario 6

Non-USD Cross Rates (Base/USD)   In the previous example, the USD was the base currency in the conversion pair (USD/JPY). In Figure 8.7 USD is the quote currency of the conversion pair (GBP/USD).

The Conversion Rate entry in Figure 8.7 is the current price of the GBP/USD pair. The reversal of the role of the U.S. dollar in the conversion pair (GBP/USD) requires another change in the profit formula:

Profit in USD = Price Change × Units Traded × Rate

or

$$\$19.05 = 0.0018 \times 20000 \times 1.8902$$

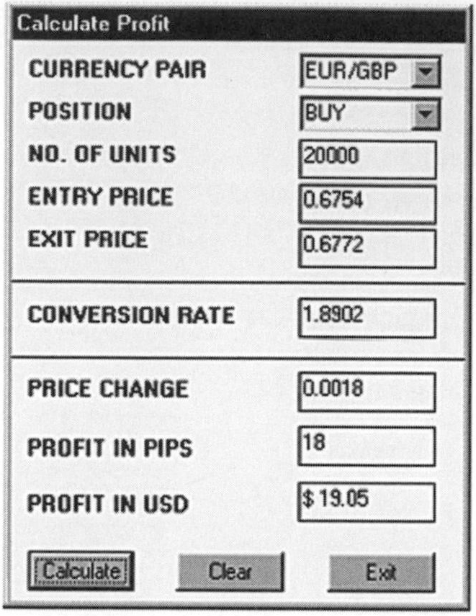

```
┌──────────────────────────────────────────┐
│ Calculate Profit                           │
│ ┌────────────────────────────────────────┐│
│ │ CURRENCY PAIR      [EUR/GBP ▼]          ││
│ │ POSITION           [BUY      ▼]          ││
│ │ NO. OF UNITS       [20000]              ││
│ │ ENTRY PRICE        [0.6754]             ││
│ │ EXIT PRICE         [0.6772]             ││
│ ├────────────────────────────────────────┤│
│ │ CONVERSION RATE    [1.8902]             ││
│ ├────────────────────────────────────────┤│
│ │ PRICE CHANGE       [0.0018]             ││
│ │ PROFIT IN PIPS     [18]                 ││
│ │ PROFIT IN USD      [$ 19.05]            ││
│ │ [Calculate]   [Clear]      [Exit]       ││
│ └────────────────────────────────────────┘│
└──────────────────────────────────────────┘
```

FIGURE 8.7   An 18-pip profit in EUR/GBP.

Remember that when USD is the quote currency of the conversion pair, you must multiply the rate. If USD is the base currency of the conversion pair, then divide the rate. Give yourself an A+ if you understood the previous examples on the first reading. You are destined for great things.

You may have noticed there was no mention of transaction costs in the six scenarios given. The broker always subtracts the transaction cost at the moment the trade is initiated; therefore transaction costs do not affect the above calculations.

Calculating Units Available

Before initiating a new trade, it is always advantageous to know the maximum number of units that you can safely trade without risking a margin call based upon your current account balance. Most trading platforms provide an online utility that calculates this information, usually resembling what is shown in Figure 8.8.

Enter the following data fields to calculate the maximum number of units to buy or sell:

- **Margin available.** This is the amount in your margin account you want to earmark for the current trade.

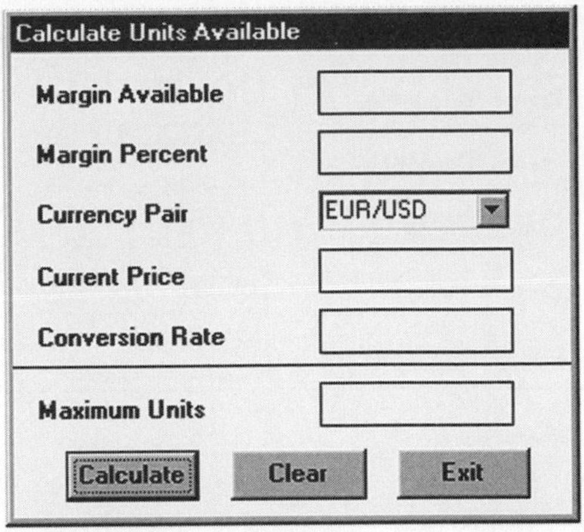

FIGURE 8.8   Units available calculator.

- **Margin percent.** This is your broker's margin percentage for leveraging trades.
- **Currency pair.** Select the corresponding currency pair. In this example, select EUR/USD.
- **Current price.** Enter the current ask price in the currency pair.
- **Conversion rate.** If the quote currency in the selected currency pair is USD, then enter "1".

Click "Calculate." (See Figure 8.9.)

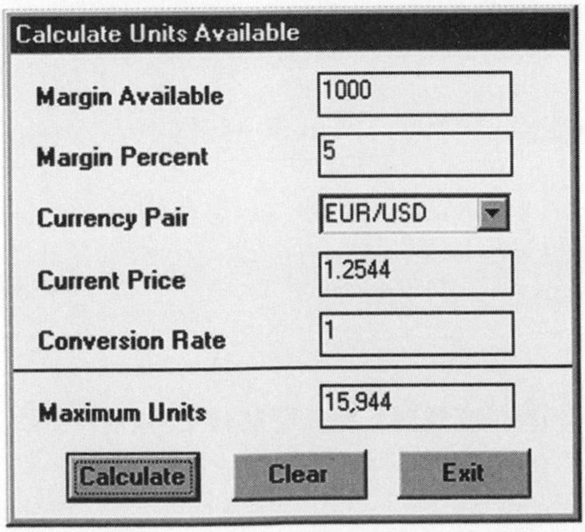

FIGURE 8.9   15,944 units available.

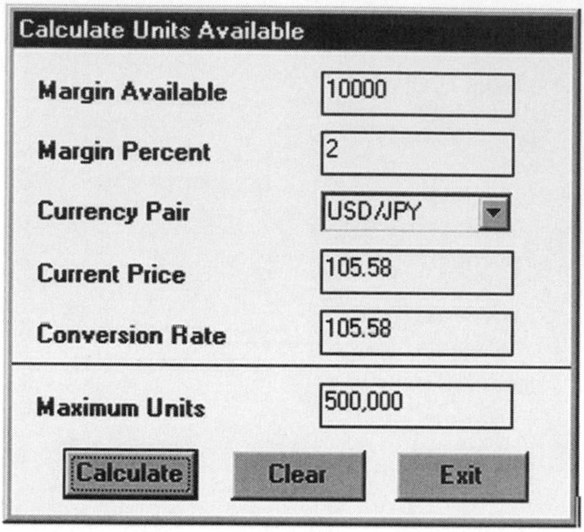

FIGURE 8.10   500,000 units available.

You can safely trade 15,000 units of EUR/USD in this example. In the next example (Figure 8.10), we calculate the units available for a currency pair in which the base currency is USD. Enter the first four fields as in the previous example. Since USD is the base currency in the USD/JPY pair, we must enter the current price as the conversion rate.

The formula to calculate the maximum units that can be traded is:

$$\text{Units Available} = 100 \times \text{Margin Available} \times \text{Rate} / (\text{Current Price} \times \text{Margin Percent})$$

If USD is the base currency, then this reduces to:

$$\text{Units Available} = 100 \times \text{Margin Available} / \text{Margin Percent}$$

Cross rates can be handled in the same fashion by simply manipulating the conversion rate. *Note:* Always decrease the unites available slightly to avoid a margin call. We recommend 10 percent.

Calculating Margin Requirements

Before executing any trade, you should always have a rough idea of how much of your account balance will be used as the margin requirement. Any trade whose margin requirement exceeds your existing account balance will not be executed. Trades whose margin requirements deplete nearly all the equity in your account are very risky and may incur the dreaded margin call. The formula to calculate the margin requirement for a trade is very simple:

$$\text{Margin Requirement} = \text{Current Price} \times \text{Units Traded} \times \text{Margin Percent} / 100$$

Assume your broker mandates a 5percent margin percentage. You want to buy a full lot (100,000 units) of the EUR/USD currency pair, which is trading at 1.2538. Thus:

$$\$6,269.00 = 1.2538 \times 100,000 \times 5 / 100$$

This trade requires $6,269.00 for margin. Proceed accordingly.

Calculating Transaction Cost

Your broker will always calculate the transaction cost because that cost is automatically subtracted from your account balance the instant you initiate a new trade. Nonetheless, it is useful to know just how the broker computes this debit. See Figure 8.11.

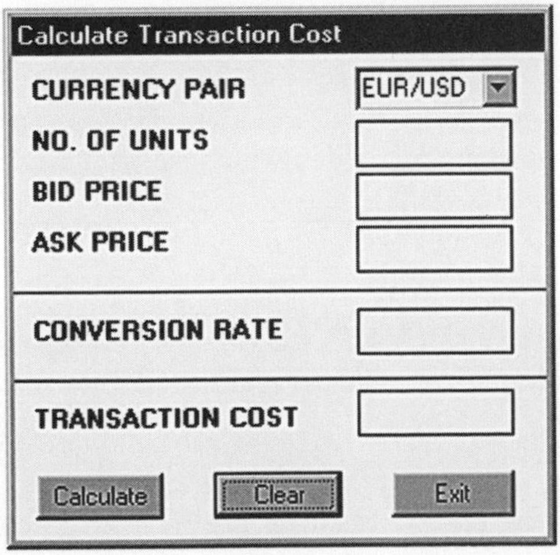

FIGURE 8.11 Calculate transaction cost.

```
┌─────────────────────────────────────────────┐
│ Calculate Transaction Cost                    │
├─────────────────────────────────────────────┤
│  CURRENCY PAIR        │EUR/USD  ▼│            │
│  NO. OF UNITS         │10000     │            │
│  BID PRICE            │1.2566    │            │
│  ASK PRICE            │1.2569    │            │
│                                               │
│  CONVERSION RATE      │1         │            │
│                                               │
│  TRANSACTION COST     │$ 3.00    │            │
│   [Calculate]    [Clear]    [Exit]            │
└─────────────────────────────────────────────┘
```

FIGURE 8.12   A 3-pip spread in EUR/USD.

Remember that the bid price is used when the trader initiates a new buy (long) trade and the ask price is used when the trader initiates a new sell (short) trade. When the USD is the quote currency in the currency pair, the conversion rate equals 1, as seen in Figure 8.12.

The basic formulas for the transaction cost in this instance are:

$$\text{Spread} = \text{Ask Price} - \text{Bid Price}$$

$$\text{Transaction Cost} = \text{Spread} \times \text{Units Traded}$$

$$\$3.00 = (1.2569 - 1.2566) \times 10{,}000$$

Figure 8.13 shows an example in which we calculate the transaction cost when the base currency is USD.

In this case, the formula becomes:

$$\text{Spread} = \text{Ask Price} - \text{Bid Price}$$

$$\text{Transaction Cost} = \text{Spread} \times \text{Units Traded} / \text{Ask Price}$$

$$\$3.24 = (1.2359 - 1.2355) \times 10{,}000 / 1.2359$$

In our final example, we calculate the transaction cost in U.S. dollars for a non-USD cross rate. We need to look up the current price of the currency pair containing USD and the quote currency of the cross rate pair (see Figure 8.14).

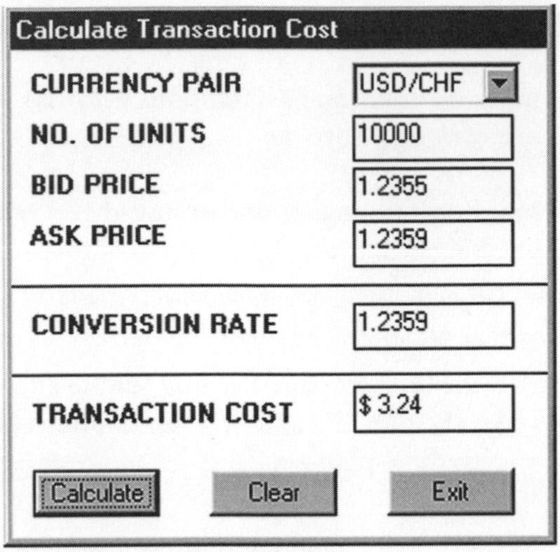

FIGURE 8.13　A 4-pip spread in USD/CHF.

In this case of non-USD cross rates, the formula becomes:

Transaction Cost = Spread × Units Traded / Conversion Rate

or

$$\$5.69 = (85.52 - 85.46) \times 10000 / 105.43$$

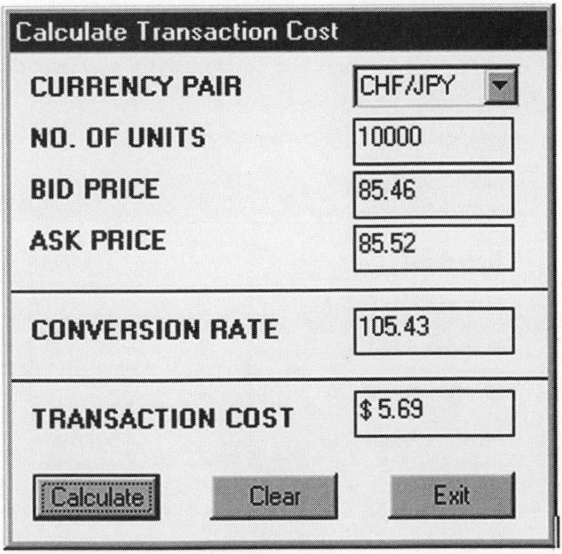

FIGURE 8.14　A 6-pip spread in CHF/JPY.

Calculating Account Summary Balance

In this section, we make the following assumptions before walking you through the accounting system of your first trade:

- You have read and thoroughly understand the FOREX trading terms described in Chapter 4.
- You have researched a half dozen or so reputable FOREX brokers and selected one that satisfies your financial needs and goals.
- You have used the broker's paper trading feature and/or the demo program that he or she provides and now feel comfortable with the screen layout of the trading platform and its mouse/keyboard navigation system.
- You have opened a new margin account, signed and returned the necessary application forms, and deposited 5,000 USD with the broker.

You are now ready to make your first trade in the FOREX currency markets. The Account Summary section of your broker's trading platform should look similar to what is shown in Figure 8.15.

Let us say that your new broker offers 20:1 leverage, which means that you must "risk" five percent of the total value of any trade that you execute, long or short. Assume that you have analyzed, both technically and fundamentally, several major currency pairs and feel that the USD/JPY pair is overpriced and it will decline in the immediate future. You now execute a very conservative entry order to sell 5,000 units of USD/JPY at a market price of 105.64. The transaction cost (the difference between the bid and the ask price) is three pips for the USD/JPY pair.

ACCOUNT SUMMARY (USD)	
Balance	5,000.00
Unrealized P & L	
Realized P & L	
Margin Used	
Margin Available	5,000.00

FIGURE 8.15   Account summary before first trade.

```
ACCOUNT SUMMARY (USD)

    Balance                    5,000.00
    Unrealized P & L              -1.42
    Realized P & L
    Margin Used                  250.00
    Margin Available           4,750.00
```

FIGURE 8.16 Account summary after market entry.

In Figure 8.16 we see that the Balance and the Realized P&L entries are unchanged. Unrealized P&L show a negative 1.42 USD. This is the round-turn transaction cost, which is subtracted the moment a new trade is executed. Each pip in the USD/JPY trade is worth 0.4733 USD. Therefore:

$$1 \text{ pip} = .1/105.64 \times 50$$

$$1 \text{ pip} = 0.4733 \text{ USD}$$

$$3 \text{ pips} = 1.4199 \text{ USD}$$

The Margin Used entry shows 250.00 USD, calculated as follows:

$$\text{Margin Used} = \text{Total Cost of Trade} \times \text{Margin Percentage}$$

$$250.00 = 5,000.00 \times 5\%$$

The Margin Available entry has also changed:

$$\text{Margin Available} = \text{Balance} - \text{Margin Used}$$

$$4,750.00 = 5,000.00 - 250.00$$

After ten minutes or so, we notice that your "feeling"—that the USD/JPY pair was oversold and would decline—has paid off. The USD/JPY has dropped to 105.51. Not only have you recouped the transaction cost (minus three pips) but you gained a plus 10 pips in profit, as shown in Figure 8.17.

At this point, market activity slows down and the price direction starts moving laterally. You decide that a plus 10 pips on your first trade is satisfactory

ACCOUNT SUMMARY (USD)	
Balance	5,000.00
Unrealized P & L	4.73
Realized P & L	
Margin Used	250.00
Margin Available	4,750.00

FIGURE 8.17   A 10-pip profit.

and you close the trade. Essentially, this means purchasing 5,000 units of USD/JPY to offset your previous sale. Once your trade liquidation is logged at the broker's firm, your new Account Summary should resemble what is shown in Figure 8.18.

The example, of course, is merely an illustration. Your first trade may be greater or smaller than the example.

For Futures Traders

Futures traders tend to think in dollars versus a commodity asset (silver, soybeans, pork bellies, etc.). The switch to corelational values—one currency against another—can be a bit trying at first. The trick is to practice calculating profit and loss for fictitious trades. Most broker dealing platforms provide such a calculator.

ACCOUNT SUMMARY (USD)	
Balance	5,004.73
Unrealized P & L	
Realized P & L	4.73
Margin Used	
Margin Available	5,004.73

FIGURE 8.18   After liquidating first trade.

In Review

The math in this chapter is not nearly as complex as it may appear at first. In fact we can reduce it all to the following cheat sheet:

$$\text{Price Change} = \text{Exit Price} - \text{Entry Price}$$

$$\text{Leverage} = 100 \,/\, \text{Margin Percent}$$

$$\text{Margin Percent} = 100 \,/\, \text{Leverage}$$

$$\text{Profit in Pips} = \text{Price Change} \times \text{Pip Factor}$$

If the Quote Currency in a trade = USD, then

$$\text{Profit in USD} = \text{Price Change} \times \text{Units Traded}$$

If the Base Currency in a trade = USD, then

$$\text{Profit in USD} = \text{Price Change} \times \text{Units Traded} \,/\, \text{Exit Price}$$

When the profit for non-USD cross rates is being calculated, the following applies:

The conversion rate is the currency pair with the USD and the quote currency of the cross rate pair.

If the quote currency of the conversion rate = USD, then

$$\text{Profit in USD} = \text{Price Change} \times \text{Units Traded} \,/\, \text{Conversion Rate}$$

If the base currency of the conversion rate = USD, then

$$\text{Profit in USD} = \text{Price Change} \times \text{Units Traded} \times \text{Conversion Rate}$$

You can now calculate profit and loss during open positions.

How to Beat the Market (Maybe)

Chapter

9

Fundamental Analysis

I t is commonly accepted that there are two major schools when formulating a trading strategy for any market, be it securities, futures, or currencies. These two disciplines are called fundamental analysis and technical analysis. The former is based on economic factors while the latter is concerned with price actions. Of course, the trader may opt to include elements of both disciplines while honing his or her personal trading strategy.

Supply and Demand

Fundamental analysis is a study of the economy and is based on the assumption that the supply and demand for currencies is a result of economic processes that can be observed in practice and that can be predicted. Fundamental analysis studies the relationship between the evolution of exchange rates and economic indicators, a relationship which it verifies and uses to make predictions.

For currencies, a fundamental trading strategy consists of strategic assessments in which a certain currency is traded based on virtually any criteria excluding the price action. These criteria include, but are not limited to, the economic condition of the country that the currency represents, monetary policy, and other elements that are fundamental to economies.

The focus of fundamental analysis lies in the economic, social, and political forces that drive supply and demand. There is no single set of beliefs that guides fundamental analysis, yet most fundamental analysts look at various macroeconomic indicators, such as economic growth rates, interest rates, inflation, and unemployment. Several theories prevail as to how currencies should be valued.

Done alone, fundamental analysis can be stressful for traders who deal with commodities, currencies, and other "margined" products. The reason for this is that fundamental analysis often does not provide specific entry and exit points, and therefore it can be difficult for traders to control risk when utilizing leverage techniques.

Currency prices are a reflection of the balance between supply and demand for currencies. Interest rates and the overall strength of the economy are the two primary factors that affect supply and demand. Economic indicators (for example, gross domestic product, foreign investment, and the trade balance) reflect the overall health of an economy. Therefore, they are responsible for the underlying changes in supply and demand for a particular currency. A tremendous amount of data relating to these indicators is released at regular intervals, and some of this data is significant. Data that is related to interest rates and international trade is analyzed very closely.

Interest Rates

If there is an uncertainty in the market in terms of interest rates, then any developments regarding interest rates can have a direct effect on the currency markets. Generally, when a country raises its interest rates, the country's currency strengthens in relation to other currencies as assets are shifted away from it to gain a higher return elsewhere. Interest rates hikes, however, are usually not good news for stock markets. This is due to the fact that many investors withdraw money from a country's stock market when there is an increase in interest rates, causing the country's currency to weaken. See Figure 9.1.

Knowing which effect prevails can be tricky, but usually there is an agreement among practitioners in the field as to what the interest rate move will do. The producer price index, the consumer price index, and the gross domestic product have proven to be the indicators with the biggest impact. The timing of interest rate moves is usually known in advance. It is generally known that these moves take place after regular meetings of the BOE (Bank of England), FED (U.S. Federal Reserve), ECB (European Central Bank), BOJ (Bank of Japan), and other central banks.

Balance of Trade

The trade balance portrays the net difference (over a period of time) between the imports and exports of a nation. When the value of imports becomes more than that of exports, the trade balance shows a deficit (this is, for the most part,

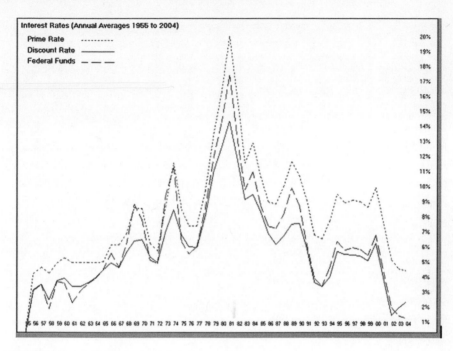

Interest Rates (Annual Averages 1955 to 2004)

Prime Rate ....
Discount Rate ————
Federal Funds — — —

FIGURE 9.1 U.S. interest rates.

considered unfavorable). For example, if Euros are sold for other domestic national currencies, such as U.S. dollars, to pay for imports, the value of the currency will depreciate due to the flow of dollars outside the country. By contrast, if trade figures show an increase in exports, money will flow into the country and increase the value of the currency. In some ways, however, a deficit is not necessarily a bad thing. A deficit is only negative if the deficit is greater than market expectations and therefore will trigger a negative price movement. See Table 9.1

TABLE 9.1 U.S. Balance of Trade, 2003 (in thousands of U.S. dollars)			
Country	Exports	Imports	Balance
China	28,418.5	152,379.1	−123,960.6
Japan	52,063.7	118,029.0	−65,965.3
Canada	169,768.8	224,165.3	−54,396.5
Mexico	97,457.3	138,073.5	−40,616.2
Germany	28,847.9	68,047.1	−39,199.2
Italy	10,569.9	25,436.6	−14,866.7
Taiwan	17,487.9	31,599.9	−14,112.0

(continued on next page)

TABLE 9.1 *(continued)*			
Country	Exports	Imports	Balance
Saudi Arabia	4,595.9	18,069.1	−13,473.2
South Korea	24,098.6	36,963.3	−12,864.7
France	17,068.2	29,221.2	−12,153.0
Thailand	5,841.8	15,180.8	−9,339.0
United Kingdom	33,895.7	42,666.9	−8,771.2
India	4,986.4	13,052.7	−8,066.3
Sweden	3,225.5	11,124.7	−7,899.2
Indonesia	2,520.1	9,520.0	−6,999.9
Russia	2,450.0	8,598.4	−6,148.4
Israel	6,878.4	12,770.3	−5,891.9
Norway	1,467.5	5,212.2	−3,744.7
Austria	1,792.6	4,489.3	−2,696.7
Denmark	1,548.3	3,718.5	−2,170.2
Philippines	7,992.1	10,061.0	−2,068.9
Switzerland	8,660.0	10,667.8	−2,007.8
Finland	1,713.8	3,597.9	−1,884.1
South Africa	2,821.3	4,637.6	−1,816.3
Hungary	934.1	2,699.2	−1,765.1
Portugal	863.0	1,967.3	−1,104.3
Turkey	2,904.3	3,788.0	−883.7
Kuwait	1,509.0	2,276.8	−767.8
Spain	5,935.3	6,708.1	−772.8
Czech Republic	672.3	1,394.4	−722.1
Poland	758.7	1,325.8	−567.1
Lichtenstein	15.9	261.9	−246.0
Iceland	242.2	283.0	−40.8
Albania	9.8	4.4	5.4
North Korea	7.9	0.1	7.8
Luxembourg	279.0	265.0	14.0
Greece	1,191.3	616.2	575.1
Singapore	16,575.8	15,158.0	1,417.8
Hong Kong	13,542.1	8,850.2	4,691.9
Belgium	15,217.9	10,140.6	5,077.3
Australia	13,103.8	6,413.9	6,689.9
Netherlands	20,703.0	10,971.8	9,731.2

Source: FTDWebMaster, Foreign Trade Division, U.S. Census Bureau, Washington, D.C.

Purchasing Power Parity

Purchasing power parity (PPP) is a theory that states that exchange rates between currencies are in equilibrium when their purchasing power is the same in each of the two countries. This means that the exchange rate between two countries should equal the ratio of the two countries' price level of a fixed basket of goods and services. When a country's domestic price level is increasing (i.e., a country experiences inflation), that country's exchange rate must depreciate in order to return to PPP.

The basis for PPP is the "law of one price." In the absence of transportation and other transaction costs, competitive markets will equalize the price of an identical good in two countries when the prices are expressed in the same currency. For example, a particular TV set that sells for 500 U.S. dollars (USD) in Seattle should cost 750 Canadian dollars (CAD) in Vancouver when the exchange rate between Canada and the United States is 1.50 USD/CAD. If the price of the TV in Vancouver cost only 700 CAD, however, consumers in Seattle would prefer buying the TV set in Vancouver. If this process (called arbitrage) is carried out on a large scale, the American consumers buying Canadian goods will bid up the value of the Canadian dollar, thus making Canadian goods more costly to them. This process continues until the goods again have the same price. There are three caveats with this law of one price: (1) As mentioned above, transportation costs, barriers to trade, and other transaction costs can be significant. (2) There must be competitive markets for the goods and services in both countries. (3) The law of one price only applies to tradeable goods; immobile goods such as houses and many services that are local are, of course, not traded between countries.

Economists use two versions of purchasing power parity: absolute PPP and relative PPP. Absolute PPP was described in the previous paragraph; it refers to the equalization of price levels across countries. Put formally, the exchange rate between Canada and the United States ECAD/USD is equal to the price level in Canada PCAN divided by the price level in the United States PUSA. Assume that the price level ratio PCAD/PUSD implies a PPP exchange rate of 1.3 CAD per 1 USD. If today's exchange rate ECAD/USD is 1.5 CAD per 1 USD, PPP theory implies that the CAD will appreciate (get stronger) against the USD, and the USD will in turn depreciate (get weaker) against the CAD.

Relative PPP refers to rates of changes of price levels, that is, inflation rates. This proposition states that the rate of appreciation of a currency is equal to the difference in inflation rates between the foreign and the home country. For example, if Canada has an inflation rate of one percent and the United States has an inflation rate of three percent, the U.S. dollar will depreciate against the Canadian dollar by two percent per year. This proposition holds well empirically, especially when the inflation differences are large.

Symbol	Currency	PPP
CHF	Swiss Franc	+54
DKK	Danish Krone	+42
JPY	Japanese Yen	+36
SEK	Swedish Krona	+35
NOK	Norwegian Krone	+30
GBP	British Pound	+22
EUR	Euro Currency	+16
AUD	Australian Dollar	+5
NZD	New Zealand Dollar	-1
CAD	Canadian Dollar	-10
KRW	Korean Won	-38
MXN	Mexican Peso	-40
HUF	Hungarian Forint	-43
CZK	Czech Koruna	-45
PLN	Polish Zloty	-51

FIGURE 9.2 Purchasing power parity.
Source: Office for Economic Cooperation and Development

The simplest way to calculate purchasing power parity between two countries is to compare the price of a "standard" good that is, in fact, identical across countries. Every year *The Economist* magazine publishes a light-hearted version of PPP: Its "Hamburger Index" lists the price of a McDonald's hamburger in various countries around the world. More sophisticated versions of PPP look at a large number of goods and services. One of the key problems in computing a comprehensive PPP is that people in different countries consume very different sets of goods and services, making it difficult to compare the purchasing power between countries. See Figure 9.2.

Gross Domestic Product

The gross domestic product (GDP) is the total market value of all goods and services produced either by domestic or foreign companies within a country's borders. GDP indicates the pace at which a country's economy is growing (or shrinking) and is considered the broadest indicator of economic output and growth.

GDPs of different countries may be compared (see Table 9.2) by converting their value in national currency according to either (a) exchange rates prevailing on international currency markets, or (b) the purchasing power parity (PPP) of each currency relative to a selected standard (usually the U.S. dollar).

The relative ranking of countries may differ dramatically depending upon which approach is used: Using official exchange rates can routinely understate the relative effective domestic purchasing power of the average producer or consumer within a less-developed economy by 50 to 60 percent, owing to the weakness of local currencies on world markets.

TABLE 9.2 Gross Domestic Product, PPP Basis

Rank Entity	PPP total USD (billions)	PPP/capita USD	Population 2003 est.
1. European Union	10,840	28,600	379,000,000
2. USA	10,400	37,600	290,343,000
3. China	5,700	4,400	1,287,000,000
4. Japan	3,550	28,000	127,215,000
5. India	2,660	2,540	1,049,701,000
6. Germany	2,180	26,600	82,399,000
7. France	1,540	25,700	60,181,000
8. United Kingdom	1,520	25,300	60,095,000
9. Italy	1,440	25,000	57,998,000
10. Russia	1,350	9,300	144,526,000
11. Brazil	1,340	7,600	182,032,000
12. South Korea	931	19,400	48,249,000
13. Canada	923	29,400	32,207,000
14. Mexico	900	9,000	104,908,000
15. Spain	828	20,700	40,218,000
16. Indonesia	663	3,100	234,894,000
17. Australia	528	27,000	19,732,000
18. Turkey	468	7,000	68,110,000
19. Iran	456	7,000	68,279,000
20. Netherlands	434	26,900	16,151,000
21. South Africa	432	10,000	42,769,000
22. Thailand	429	6,900	70,000,000
23. Taiwan	406	18,000	22,116,000
24. Argentina	391	10,200	38,000,000
25. Poland	368	9,500	38,000,000

Source: CIA World Factbook: PPP, PPP/Capita, Population

However, comparison based on official exchange rates can offer a better indication of a country's purchasing power on the international market for goods and services.

Intervention

Another important fundamental influence on FOREX currency prices is called intervention. This occurs when an official regulatory agency or a financial institution with one government directly coerces the exchange rate of its currency, usually by reevaluation, devaluation, or by the manipulation of imports and exports in some way.

Such actions may cause broad and erratic changes in the exchange rate with foreign currencies. However, it is from such anomalies that the FOREX trader may profit, if the proper stop-loss safeguards are in place.

Other Economic Indicators

Industrial Production

Industrial production (IP) is a chain-weighted measure of the change in the production of the nation's factories, mines, and utilities, as well as a measure of their industrial capacity and how many available resources among factories, utilities, and mines are being used (commonly known as capacity utilization). The manufacturing sector accounts for one-quarter of the economy. The capacity utilization rate provides an estimate of how much factory capacity is in use.

Purchasing Managers Index

The National Association of Purchasing Managers (NAPM), now called the Institute for Supply Management, releases a monthly composite index of national manufacturing conditions, constructed from data on new orders, production, supplier delivery times, backlogs, inventories, prices, employment, export orders, and import orders. It is divided into manufacturing and non-manufacturing subindices.

Producer Price Index

The producer price index (PPI) is a measure of price changes in the manufacturing sector. It measures average changes in selling prices received by domestic producers in the manufacturing, mining, agriculture, and electric utility industries for their output. The PPIs most often used for economic analysis are those for finished goods, intermediate goods, and crude goods.

Consumer Price Index

The consumer price index (CPI) is a measure of the average price level paid by urban consumers (80 percent of the population) for a fixed basket of goods and services. It reports price changes in over 200 categories. The CPI also includes various user fees and taxes directly associated with the prices of specific goods and services.

Durable Goods

The durable goods orders indicator measures new orders placed with domestic manufacturers for immediate and future delivery of factory hard goods. A durable good is defined as a good that lasts an extended period of time (over three years) during which its services are extended.

Employment Cost Index

Payroll employment is a measure of the number of jobs in more than 500 industries in all 50 states and 255 metropolitan areas. The employment estimates are based on a survey of larger businesses and count the number of paid employees working part-time or full-time in the nation's business and government establishments.

Retail Sales

The retail sales report is a measure of the total receipts of retail stores from samples representing all sizes and kinds of business in retail trade throughout the nation. It is the timeliest indicator of broad consumer spending patterns and is adjusted for normal seasonal variation, holidays, and trading-day differences. Retail sales include durable and nondurable merchandise sold, and services and excise taxes incidental to the sale of merchandise. Excluded are sales taxes collected directly from the customer.

Housing Starts

The housing starts report measures the number of residential units on which construction is begun each month. A start in construction is defined as the beginning of excavation of the foundation for the building and is comprised primarily of residential housing. Housing is very interest rate–sensitive and is one of the first sectors to react to changes in interest rates. Significant reaction of starts/permits to changing interest rates signals that interest rates are nearing a trough or a peak. To analyze the data, focus on the percentage change in levels from the previous month. The report is released around the middle of the following month.

Forecasting

Fundamental analysis refers to the study of the core underlying elements that influence the economy of a particular entity. It is a method of study that attempts to predict price action and market trends by analyzing economic indicators, government policy, and societal factors (to name just a few elements) within a business cycle framework. If you think of the financial markets as a big clock, the fundamentals are the gears and springs that move the hands around the face. Anyone walking down the street can look at this clock and tell you what time it is now, but the fundamentalist can tell you how it came to be this time and more importantly, what time (or more precisely, what price) it will be in the future.

There is a tendency to pigeonhole traders into two distinct schools of market analysis—fundamental and technical. Indeed, the first question posed to you after you tell someone that you are a trader is generally "Are you a technician or a fundamentalist?" The reality is that it has become increasingly difficult to be a purist of either persuasion. Fundamentalists need to keep an eye on the various signals derived from the price action on charts, while few technicians can afford to completely ignore impending economic data, critical political decisions, or the myriad of societal issues that influence prices.

Bearing in mind that the financial underpinnings of any country, trading bloc, or multinational industry take into account many factors, including social, political, and economic influences, staying on top of an extremely fluid fundamental picture can be challenging. At the same time, you'll find that your knowledge and understanding of a dynamic global market will increase immeasurably as you delve further and further into the complexities and subtleties of the fundamentals of the markets.

Fundamental analysis is a very effective way to forecast economic conditions, but not necessarily exact market prices. For example, when analyzing an economist's forecast of the upcoming GDP or employment report, you begin to get a fairly clear picture of the general health of the economy and the forces at work behind it. However, you'll need to come up with a precise method as to how best to translate this information into entry and exit points for a particular trading strategy.

A trader who studies the markets using fundamental analysis generally creates models to formulate a trading strategy. These models typically utilize a host of empirical data and attempt to forecast market behavior and estimate future values or prices by using past values of core economic indicators. These forecasts are then used to derive specific trades that best exploit this information.

Forecasting models are as numerous and varied as the traders and market buffs that create them. Two people can look at the same data and come up with two completely different conclusions about how the market will be influenced by it. Therefore it is important that before casting yourself into a particular mold regarding any aspect of market analysis, you study the fundamentals and see how they best fit your trading style and expectations.

Do not succumb to "paralysis by analysis." Given the multitude of factors that fall under the heading of "The Fundamentals," there is a distinct danger of information overload. Sometimes traders fall into this trap and are unable to pull the trigger on a trade. This is one of the reasons why many traders turn to technical analysis. To some, technical analysis is seen as a way to transform all of the fundamental factors that influence the markets into one simple tool: prices. However, trading a particular market without knowing a great deal about the exact nature of its underlying elements is like fishing without bait. You might get lucky and snare a few on occasion, but it's not the best approach over the long haul.

For FOREX traders, the fundamentals are everything that makes a country tick. From interest rates and central bank policy to natural disasters, the fundamentals are a dynamic mix of distinct plans, erratic behaviors, and unforeseen events. Therefore, it is easier to get a handle on the most influential contributors to this diverse mix than it is to formulate a comprehensive list of all the fundamentals.

Economic indicators are snippets of financial and economic data published by various agencies of the government or private sector. These statistics, which are made public on a regularly scheduled basis, help market observers monitor the pulse of the economy. Therefore, they are religiously followed by almost everyone in the financial markets. With so many people poised to react to the same information, economic indicators in general have tremendous potential to generate volume and to move prices in the markets. While on the surface it might seem that an advanced degree in economics would come in handy to analyze and then trade on the glut of information contained in these economic indicators, a few simple guidelines are all that is necessary to track, organize, and make trading decisions based on the data.

Know exactly when each economic indicator is due to be released. Keep a calendar on your desk or trading station that contains the date and time when each statistic will be made public. You can find these calendars on the N.Y. Federal Reserve Bank Web site using this link: *http://www.ny.frb.org/*. Then search for "economic indicators." The same information is also available from many other sources on the Web or from the company you use to execute your trades.

Keeping track of the calendar of economic indicators will also help you make sense out of otherwise unanticipated price action in the market. Consider this scenario: It's Monday morning and the U.S. dollar has been in a tailspin for three weeks. As such, it is safe to assume that many traders are holding large short USD positions. However, the employment data for the United States is due to be released on Friday. It is very likely that with this key piece of economic information soon to be made public, the USD could experience a short-term rally leading up to the data on Friday as traders pare down their short positions.

The point here is that economic indicators can affect prices directly (following their release to the public) or indirectly (as traders massage their positions in anticipation of the data).

Understand which particular aspect of the economy is being revealed in the data. For example, you should know which indicators measure the growth of the economy (GDP) versus those that measure inflation (PPI, CPI) or employment (non-farm payrolls). After you follow the data for a while, you will become very familiar with the nuances of each economic indicator and which part of the economy it measures.

Not all economic indicators are created equal. Well, they might have been created with equal importance but along the way, some have acquired much greater potential to move the markets than others. Market participants will place higher regard on one statistic versus another depending on the state of the economy.

Know which indicators the markets are keying on. For example, if prices (inflation) are not a crucial issue for a particular country, the markets will probably not as keenly anticipate or react to inflation data. However, if economic growth is a vexing problem, changes in employment data or GDP will be eagerly anticipated and could precipitate tremendous volatility following its release.

The data itself is not as important as whether or not it falls within market expectations. Besides knowing when all the data will hit the wires, it is vitally important that you know what economists and other market pundits are forecasting for each indicator. For example, knowing the economic consequences of an unexpected monthly rise of 0.3 percent in the producer price index (PPI) is not nearly as vital to your short-term trading decisions as it is to know that this month the market was looking for PPI to fall by 0.1 percent. As mentioned, you should know that PPI measures prices and that an unexpected rise could be a sign of inflation. But analyzing the longer-term ramifications of this unexpected monthly rise in prices can wait until after you have taken advantage of the trading opportunities presented by the data. Once again, market expectations for all economic releases are published on various sources on the Web and you should post these expectations on your calendar along with the release date of the indicator.

Do not get caught up in the headlines, however. Part of getting a handle on what the market is forecasting for various economic indicators is knowing the key aspects of each indicator. While your macroeconomics professor might have drilled the significance of the unemployment rate into your head, even junior traders can tell you that the headline figure is for amateurs and that the most closely watched detail in the payroll data is the non-farm payrolls figure. Other economic indicators are similar in that the headline figure is not nearly as closely watched as the finer points of the data. PPI, for example, measures changes in producer prices. But the statistic most closely watched by the markets is PPI, minus food and energy price changes. Traders know that the food and energy component of the data is much too volatile and subject to revisions on a month-to-month basis to provide an accurate reading on the changes in producer prices.

Speaking of revisions, do not be too quick to pull that trigger should a particular economic indicator fall outside of market expectations. Contained in each new economic indicator released to the public are revisions to previously released data. For example, if durable goods should rise by 0.5 percent in the current month, while the market is anticipating them to fall, the unexpected rise could be the result of a downward revision to the prior month. Look at revisions to older data because in this case, the previous month's durable goods figure might have been originally reported as a rise of 0.5 percent but now, along with the new figures, it is being revised to indicate a rise of only 0.1 percent. Therefore, the unexpected rise in the current month is likely the result of a downward revision to the previous month's data.

Do not forget that there are two sides to a trade in the foreign exchange market. So, while you might have a handle on the complete package of economic indicators published in the United States or Europe, most other countries also publish similar economic data. The important thing to remember here is that not all countries are as efficient as the G8 in releasing this information. Once again, if you are going to trade the currency of a particular country, you need to find out the particulars about that country's economic indicators. As mentioned earlier, not all of these indicators carry the same weight in the markets and not all of them are as accurate as others. Do your homework so you won't be caught off guard.

When it comes to focusing exclusively on the impact that economic indicators have on price action in a particular market, the foreign exchange markets are the most challenging. Therefore, they have the greatest potential for profits of any market. Obviously, factors other than economic indicators move prices and as such make other markets more or less potentially profitable. But since a currency is a proxy for the country it represents, the economic health of that country is priced into the currency. One very important way to measure the health of an economy is through economic indicators. The challenge comes in diligently keeping track of the nuts and bolts of each country's particular economic information package. Here are a few general comments about economic indicators and some of the more closely watched data.

Most economic indicators can be divided into leading and lagging indicators. Leading indicators are economic factors that change before the economy starts to follow a particular pattern or trend. Leading indicators are used to predict changes in the economy. Lagging indicators are economic factors that change after the economy has already begun to follow a particular pattern or trend.

The problem with fundamental analysis is that it is difficult to convert the "qualitative" information into a specific price prediction. With FOREX leverage being what it is, it is seldom enough to know that a report is "bullish" for a currency without being able to attach specific values.

Even if you opt for a technical analysis trading approach, as most traders do, *do not* completely ignore the fundamentals. Use a new service to do a daily take on what's happening. Remember: Be aware of pending reports, statistical releases, and so on, as they often will cause a violent market reaction one way or the other.

The authors consulted numerous sources while compiling the current chapter. We wish to acknowledge specifically *http://www.sbfx.net/fundamental_analysis. aspx* for their informative Web site. Fundamental analysis is a very deep well. It is important to understand the basic fundamentals that drive currency prices, even though most traders use technical analysis to make specific day-to-day trading decisions.

Chapter 10

Technical Analysis

Overview

Probably the most successful and most utilized means of making decisions and analyzing FOREX markets is technical analysis. The difference between technical and fundamental analyses is that technical analysis ignores fundamental factors and is applied only to the price action of the market. While fundamental data can often provide only a long-term forecast of exchange rate movements, technical analysis has become the primary tool to successfully analyze and trade shorter-term price movements, as well as to set profit targets and stop-loss safeguards because of its ability to generate price-specific information and forecasts.

Historically, technical analysis in the futures markets has focused on the six price fields available during any given period of time: open, high, low, close, volume, and open interest. Since the FOREX market has no central exchange, it is very difficult to estimate the latter two fields, volume and open interest. In this chapter, we therefore limit our analysis to the first four price fields.

Technical analysis consists primarily of a variety of technical studies, each of which can be interpreted to predict market direction or to generate buy and sell signals. Many technical studies share one common important tool: a price-time chart that emphasizes selected characteristics in the price motion of the underlying security. One great advantage of technical analysis is its "visualness."

Bar Charts

Bar charts are the most widely used type of chart in security market technical analysis and date back to the last decade of the nineteenth century. They are popular because they are easy to construct and understand. These charts are constructed by representing intra-day, daily, weekly, or monthly activity as a vertical bar. Opening and closing prices are represented by horizontal marks to the left and right of the vertical bar respectively. Spotting both patterns and the trend of a market, two of the essentials of chart reading, is often easiest using bar charts. Bar charts present the data individually, without linking prices to neighboring prices. Each set of price fields is a single "island."

Each vertical bar has the components shown in Figure 10.1.

Figure 10.2 shows a daily bar chart for the EUR/USD currency pair for the month of June 2003. The vertical scale on the right represents the cost of one Euro in terms of U.S. dollars. The horizontal legend at the bottom of the chart represents the day of week.

A common method of classifying the vertical bars is to show the relationships between the opening and closing prices within a single time interval, as seen in Figure 10.3.

Graphically, an open/high/low/close (OHLC) bar chart is defined using the following algorithm:

OHLC Bar Chart Algorithm

- Step 1—One vertical rectangle whose upper boundary represents the high for the day and whose lower boundary represents the low for the given time period.
- Step 2—One horizontal rectangle to the left of the high-low rectangle whose central value represents the opening price for the given period.
- Step 3—One horizontal rectangle to the right of the high-low rectangle whose central value represents the closing price for the given period.

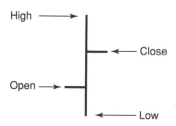

FIGURE 10.1　Anatomy of single vertical bar.

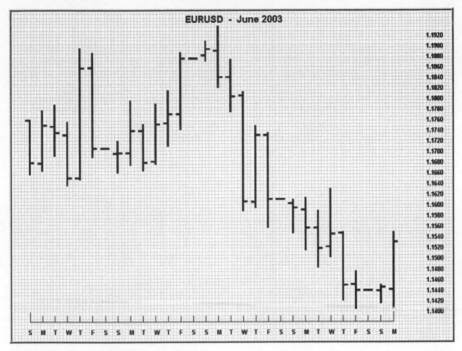

FIGURE 10.2   Vertical bar chart.

One interesting variation to the standard OHLC bar chart was developed by author/trader Burton Pugh is the 1930s. His model involved connecting the previous set of quotes to the current set of quotes, which generates a continuous line representation of price movements. There are four basic formations between two adjacent vertical bars in Burton's system. (see Figure 10.4)

Bar chart interpretation is one of the most fascinating and well-studied topics in the realm of technical analysis. Recurring bar chart formations have been labeled, categorized, and analyzed in detail. Common formations like tops, bottoms, head-and-shoulders, inverted head-and-shoulders, lines of support and resistance, reversals, and so forth, are examined in the following sections.

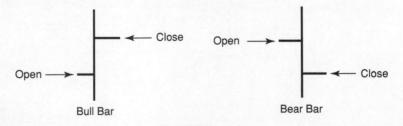

FIGURE 10.3   Anatomy of bull and bear bars.

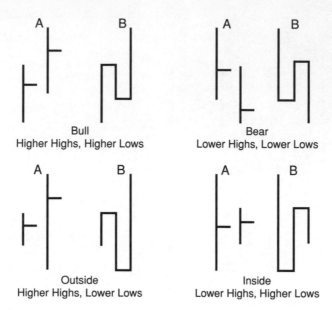

FIGURE 10.4   Continuous line bar chart.

Trend Lines

A trend can be up, down, or lateral and is represented by drawing a straight line above the daily highs in a downward trend and a straight line below the daily lows in an upward trend. See Figure 10.5

A common trading technique involves the intersection of the trend line with the most recent prices. If the trend line for a downward trend crosses

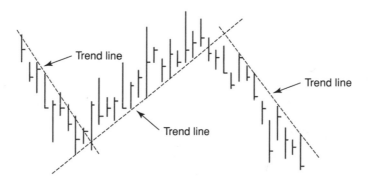

FIGURE 10.5   Bar chart with trend lines.

through the most recent prices, a buy signal is generated. Conversely, if the trend line for an upward trend passes through the most recent prices, then a sell signal is generated.

Support and Resistance

Support levels indicate the price at which most traders feel that prices will move higher. There is sufficient demand for a security to cause a halt in a downward trend and turn the trend up. You can spot support levels on the bar charts by looking for a sequence of daily lows that fluctuate only slightly along a horizontal line. When a support level is penetrated (the price drops below the support level) it often becomes a resistance level; this is because traders want to limit their losses and will sell later, when prices approach the former level.

Like support levels, resistance levels are horizontal lines on the bar chart. They mark the upper level for trading, or a price at which sellers typically outnumber buyers. When resistance levels are broken, the price moves above the resistance level, and often does so decisively. See Figure 10.6.

Many traders find lines of support and resistance useful in determining the placement of stop-loss and take-profit limit orders.

Recognizing Chart Patterns

Proper identification of an ongoing trend can be a tremendous asset to the trader. However, the trader must also learn to recognize recurring chart patterns that disrupt the continuity of trend lines. Broadly speaking, these chart patterns can be categorized as reversal patterns and continuation patterns.

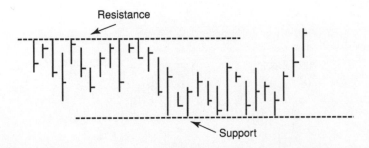

FIGURE 10.6   Bar chart with support and resistance lines.

Reversal Patterns

Reversal patterns are important because they inform the trader that a market entry point is unfolding or that it may be time to liquidate an open position. Figures 10.7 through 10.10 illustrate the most common reversal patterns.

FIGURE 10.7 Double top.

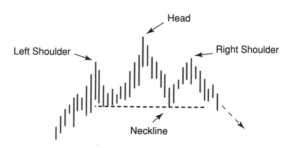

FIGURE 10.8 Double bottom.

Head

Left Shoulder

Right Shoulder

Neckline

FIGURE 10.9 Head-and-shoulders top.

FIGURE 10.10   Head-and-shoulders bottom.

Continuation Patterns

A continuation pattern implies that while a visible trend was in progress, it was temporarily interrupted, and then continued in the direction of the original trend. The most common continuation patterns are shown in Figure 10.11 through 10.15.

   The proper identification of a continuation pattern may prevent the trader from prematurely liquidating an open position that still has profit potential.

FIGURE 10.11   Flag or pennant.

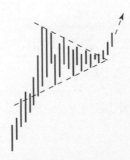

FIGURE 10.12   Symmetrical triangle.

FIGURE 10.13   Ascending triangle.

FIGURE 10.14   Descending triangle.

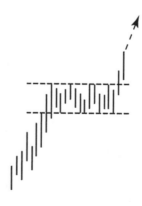

FIGURE 10.15   Rectangle.

Gaps

A gap occurs when the trading range on a given day lies outside the trading range of the previous day. Often the result of an emotional response to overnight news, a gap can be an indication of a new price trend. See Figures 10.16.through 10.19.

The authors' research indicates that gaps are of special importance in FOREX.

FIGURE 10.16 Breakaway gap.

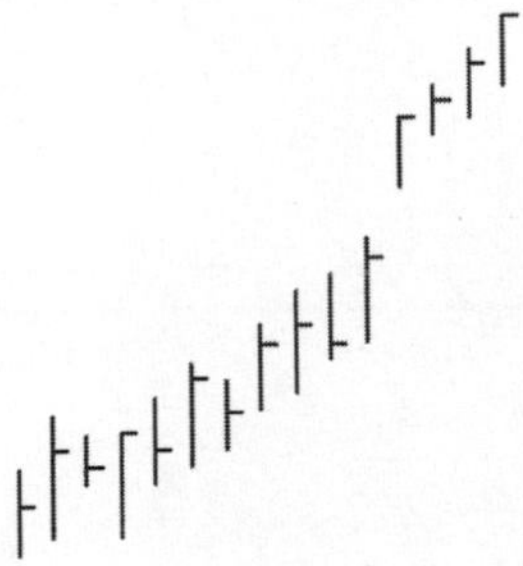

FIGURE 10.17 Runaway gap.

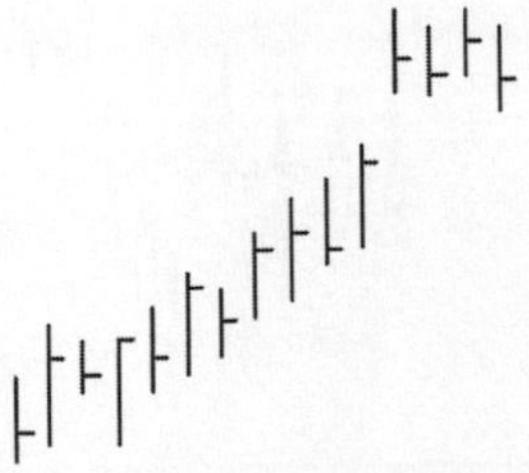

FIGURE 10.18 Exhaustion gap.

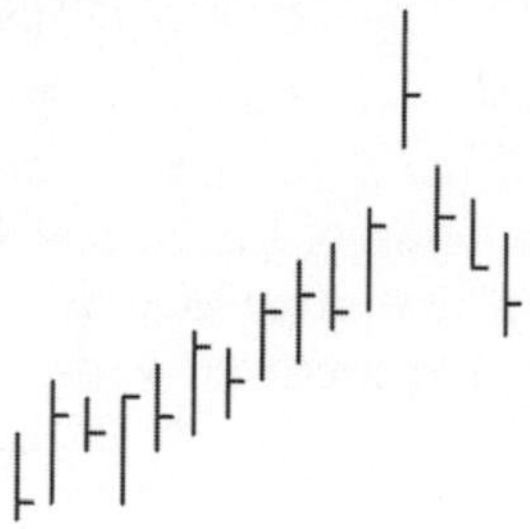

FIGURE 10.19   Island reversal gap.

Candlestick Charts

Candlestick charting is usually credited to the Japanese rice trader Munehisa Homma in the early eighteenth century, though many references indicate that this method of technical analysis probably existed as early as the 1600s. Steven Nison of Merrill Lynch is credited with popularizing candlestick charting in Western markets and has become recognized as the leading expert on their interpretation. See Figure 10.20.

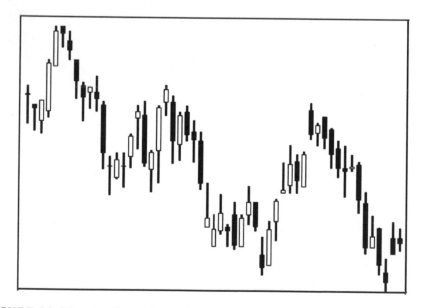

FIGURE 10.20   Candlestick chart.

The candlestick is the graphic representation of the price bar: the open, high, low, and closing price of the period. The algorithm to construct a candlestick chart follows:

Candlestick Chart Algorithm

- Step 1—The candlestick is made up of a body and two shadows.
- Step 2—The body is depicted as a vertical column bounded by the opening price and the closing price.
- Step 3—The shadows are just vertical lines—a line above the body to the high of the day (the upper shadow) and a line below the body to the low of the day (the lower shadow).
- Step 4—It is customary for the body to be empty if the close was higher than the open (a bull day) and filled if the close was lower than the open (a bear day).

The elements of a candlestick bar are shown in Figure 10.21.

The nomenclature used to identify individual or consecutive combinations of candlesticks is rich in imagery: Hammer, hanging man, dark cloud cover, morning star, three black crows, three mountains, three advanced white soldiers, and spinning tops are only a few of the candlestick patterns that have been categorized and used in technical analysis.

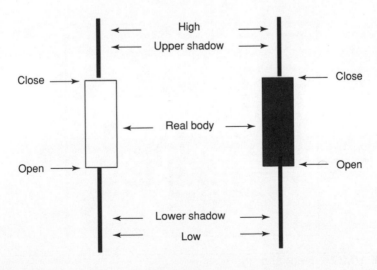

FIGURE 10.21 Anatomy of candlestick bar.

A thorough description of how to interpret candlestick charts is given in Steven Nison's books: *Japanese Candlestick Charting Techniques*, Hall, 1991, and *Beyond Candlesticks: More Japanese Charting Techniques Revealed*, Wiley, 1994. A summary of the different candlestick patterns can also be found at *www.hotcandle. com/candle.htm*.

Point and Figure Charts

The modern point and figure (P&F) chart was created in the late nineteenth century and is roughly 15 years older than the standard OHLC bar chart. This technique, also called the three-box reversal method, is probably the oldest Western method of charting prices still around today.

Its roots date back into trading lore, as it has been intimated that this method was successfully used by the legendary trader James R. Keene during the merger of U.S. Steel in 1901. Mr. Keene was employed by Andrew Carnegie to distribute the company shares, as Carnegie refused to take stock as payment for his equity interest in the company. Keene, using point and figure charting and tape readings, managed to promote the stock and get rid of Carnegie's sizeable stake without causing the price to crash. This simple method of charting has stood the test of time and requires less time to construct and maintain than the traditional bar chart. See Figure 10.22.

The point and figure method derives its name from the fact that price is recorded using figures (*X*s and *O*s) to represent a point, hence the name "Point

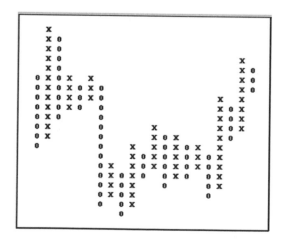

FIGURE 10.22   Point and figure chart.

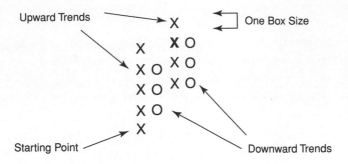

FIGURE 10.23 Anatomy of point and figure columns.

and Figure." Charles Dow, the original founder of the *Wall Street Journal* and the inventor of stock indexes, was rumored to be a point and figure user. Indeed, the practice of point and figure charting is alive and well today on the floor of all futures exchanges. The method's simplicity in identifying price trends and support and resistance levels, as well as its ease of upkeep, has allowed it to endure the test of time, even in the age of Web pages, personal computers, and the information explosion.

The elements of the point and figure anatomy are shown on Figure 10.23.

Two user-defined variables are required to plot a point and figure chart, the first of which is called the box size. This is the minimum grid increment that the price must move in order to satisfy the plotting of a new X and O. The selection of the box size variable is usually based upon a multiple of the minimum tick size determined by the commodity exchange. If the box size is too small, then the point and figure chart will not filter out white noise, while too large a filter will not present enough detail in the chart to make it useful. We recommend initializing the box size for a FOREX P&F chart with the value of one or two pips in the underlying currency pair.

The second user-defined parameter necessary to plot a point and figure chart is called the reversal amount. If the price moves in the same direction as the existing trend, then only one box size is required to plot the continuation of the trend. However, in order to filter out small fluctuations in price movements (or lateral congestion), a reversal in trend cannot be plotted until it satisfies the reversal amount constraint. Typically, this value is set at three box sizes, though any value between one and seven is a plausible candidate. The daily limit imposed by most commodity exchanges can also influence the trader's selection of the reversal amount variable.

The algorithm to construct a point and figure chart follows:

Point and Figure Algorithm

- Upward trends are represented as a vertical column of *X*s, while downward trends are displayed as an adjacent column of *O*s.

- New figures (*X*s or *O*s) cannot be added to the current column unless the increase (or decrease) in price satisfies the minimum box size requirement.

- A reversal cannot be plotted in the subsequent column until the price has changed by the reversal amount times the box size.

Point and figure charts display the underlying supply and demand of prices. A column of *X*s shows that demand is exceeding supply (a rally); a column of *O*s shows that supply is exceeding demand (a decline); and a series of short columns shows that supply and demand are relatively equal. There are several advantages to using P&F charts instead of the more traditional bar or candlestick charts.

P&F charts automatically:

Advantages of P&F Charts

- Eliminate the insignificant price movements that often make bar charts appear "noisy."

- Remove the often misleading effects of time from the analysis process (whipsawing).

- Make trend line recognition a "no-brainer."

- Make recognizing support/resistance levels much easier.

  Nearly all of the pattern formations discussed above have analogous patterns that appear when using a standard OHLC bar chart. Adjusting the two variables, box size and reversal amount, may cause these patterns to become more recognizable. P&F charts also:

- Are a viable online analytical tool in real time. They require only a sheet of paper and pencil.

- Help you stay focused on the important long-term price developments.

For a more detailed examination of this charting technique, we recommend *Point & Figure Charting* by Thomas J. Dorsey (2001: John Wiley & Sons, Inc.).

Indicators and Oscillators

Beyond charting are various market indicators—calculations using the primary information of open, high, low, or close. Indicators may also be charted or graphed. Buy and sell signals and complete systems may be generated from a battery of indicators. The most popular indicators are: relative strength, moving averages, oscillators or momentum analysis (actually a superset of relative strength), and Bollinger bands.

Relative Strength Indicator

The relative strength indicator (RSI) shows whether a currency is overbought or oversold. Overbought indicates an upward market trend, since the financial operators are buying a currency in the hope of further rate increases. Sooner or later saturation will occur because the financial operators have already created a long position. They show restraint in making additional purchases and try to make a profit. The profits made can very quickly lead to a change in the trend or at least a consolidation.

Oversold indicates that the market is showing downward trend conditions, since the operators are selling a currency in the hope of further rate falls. Over time saturation will occur because the financial operators have created short positions. They then limit their sales and try to compensate for the short positions with profits. This can rapidly lead to a change in the trend.

You cannot determine directly whether the market is overbought or oversold. This would suppose that you knew all of the foreign exchange positions of all the financial operators. However, experience shows that only speculative buying, which leads to an overbought situation, makes very rapid rate rallies possible.

The RSI is a numerical indication of price fluctuations over a given period; it is expressed as a percentage.

RSI = sum of price rises / sum of all price fluctuations

To illustrate this, we have selected the daily closes (multiplied by 10,000) for the EUR/USD currency pair when it first appeared on the FOREX market in January of 2002. The running time frame in this example is nine days. See Table 10.1.

An RSI between 30 and 70 percent is considered neutral. Below 25 percent indicates an oversold market, over 75 percent indicates an overbought market. The RSI should never be considered alone but in conjunction with other indicators and charts. Moreover, its interpretation depends largely on the period studied. The example in Table 10.1 is nine days. An RSI over 25 days would show,

TABLE 10.1		Calculating RSI				
Date	Close	Daily Chg	Ups	Downs	Total	Percent
1/01/02	8894					
1/02/02	9037	+43				
1/03/02	8985	−51				
1/04/02	8944	−41				
1/07/02	8935	−9				
1/08/02	8935	0				
1/09/02	8914	−21				
1/10/02	8914	0				
1/11/02	8925	+11	54	122	176	30.7
1/14/02	8943	+18	72	122	194	37.1
1/15/02	8828	−15	29	137	166	17.5
1/16/02	8821	−7	29	93	122	23.8
1/17/02	8814	−7	29	59	88	33.0
1/18/02	8846	+32	61	50	111	55.0
1/21/02	8836	−10	61	60	121	50.4
1/22/02	8860	+24	85	39	124	68.5
1/23/02	8783	+23	108	39	147	73.5
1/24/02	8782	−1	97	40	137	70.8
1/25/02	8650	−132	79	171	250	31.6
1/28/02	8623	−27	79	183	262	30.2
1/29/02	8656	+33	112	176	288	39.0
1/30/02	8610	−46	112	215	327	34.3
1/31/02	8584	−26	80	232	312	25.6

given a steady evolution of rates, fewer fluctuations. The advantage of obtaining more rapid signals for selling and buying (by using a smaller number of days) is counterbalanced by a greater risk of receiving the unconfirmed signals.

Momentum Analysis

Like the RSI, momentum measures the rate of change in trends over a given period. Unlike the RSI, which measures all the rate changes and fluctuations within a given period, momentum allows you to analyze only the rate variations between the start and end of the period studied.

The larger n is, the more the daily fluctuations tend to disappear. When momentum is above zero or its curve is rising, it indicates an uptrend. A signal to buy is given as soon as the momentum exceeds zero, and when it drops below zero, triggers the signal to sell.

$$\text{Momentum} = \text{price on day } (X) - \text{price on day } (X - n)$$

where n = number of days in the period studied.

The following example in Table 10.2 of momentum analysis uses the EUR/USD currency pair as the underlying security.

TABLE 10.2	Calculating Momentum	
Date	Close	9-Day Momentum
1/01/02	8894	
1/02/02	9037	
1/03/02	8985	
1/04/02	8944	
1/07/02	8935	
1/08/02	8935	
1/09/02	8914	
1/10/02	8914	
1/11/02	8925	
1/14/02	8943	+49
1/15/02	8828	−209
1/16/02	8821	−164
1/17/02	8814	−130
1/18/02	8846	−99
1/21/02	8836	−99
1/22/02	8860	−54
1/23/02	8783	−131
1/24/02	8782	−143
1/25/02	8650	−293
1/28/02	8623	−205
1/29/02	8656	−165
1/30/02	8610	−204
1/31/02	8584	−262

Examination of the nine-day momentum shows a clear downward trend. Momentum analysis should not be used as the sole criterion for market entry and exit timing, but in conjunction with other indicators and chart signals.

Moving Averages

The moving average (MA) is another instrument used to study trends and generate market entry and exit signals. It is the arithmetic average of closing prices over a given period. The longer the period studied, the weaker the magnitude of the moving average curve. The number of closes in the given period is called the moving average index.

Market signals are generated by calculating the residual value:

$$\text{Residual} = \text{Price}(X) - \text{MA}(X)$$

When the residual crosses into the positive area, a buy signal is generated. When the residual drops below zero, a sell signal is generated.

A significant refinement to this residual method (also called moving average convergence divergence, or MACD for short) is the use of two moving averages. When the MA with the shorter MA index (called the oscillating MA index) crosses above the MA with the longer MA index (called the basis MA index), a sell signal is generated.

$$\text{Residual} = \text{Basis MA}(X) - \text{Oscillating MA}(X)$$

Again we use the EUR/USD currency pair to illustrate the moving average method (see Table 10.3).

The reliability of the moving average residual method depends heavily on the MA indices chosen. Depending on market conditions, it is the shorter periods or longer periods that give the best results. When an ideal combination of moving averages is used, the results are comparatively good. The disadvantage is that the signals to buy and sell are indicated relatively late, after the maximum and minimum rates have been reached.

The residual method can be optimized by simple experimentation or by a software program. Keep in mind that when a large sample of daily closes is used, the indices will need to be adjusted as market conditions change.

Bollinger Bands

This indicator was developed by John Bollinger and is explained in detail in his opus called *Bollinger on Bollinger Bands.* The technique involves overlaying three

TABLE 10.3   Calculating Moving Average Residuals

Date	Close	3-Day MA	5-Day MA	Residual
1/01/02	8894			
1/02/02	9037			
1/03/02	8985	8972		
1/04/02	8944	8989		
1/07/02	8935	8955	8959	4
1/08/02	8935	8938	8967	29
1/09/02	8914	8928	8943	15
1/10/02	8914	8921	8928	7
1/11/02	8925	8918	8925	7
1/14/02	8943	8927	8926	−1
1/15/02	8828	8899	8905	6
1/16/02	8821	8864	8886	22
1/17/02	8814	8821	8866	45
1/18/02	8846	8827	8850	23
1/21/02	8836	8832	8829	−3
1/22/02	8860	8847	8835	−12
1/23/02	8783	8826	8828	2
1/24/02	8782	8808	8821	13
1/25/02	8650	8738	8782	44
1/28/02	8623	8685	8740	55
1/29/02	8656	8643	8699	56
1/30/02	8610	8630	8664	34
1/31/02	8584	8617	8625	8

bands (lines) on top of an OHLC bar chart (or a candlestick chart) of the underlying security.

The central band is a simple arithmetic moving average of the daily closes using a trader-selected moving average index. The upper and lower bands are the running standard deviation above and below the central moving average. Since the standard deviation is a measure of volatility, the bands are self-adjusting, widening during volatile markets and contracting during calmer periods. Bollinger recommends 10 days for short-term trading, 20 days for

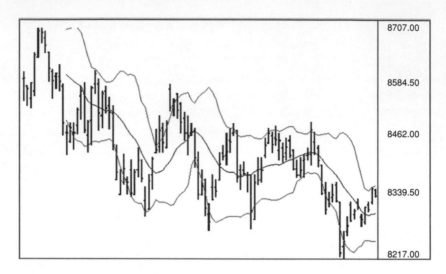

FIGURE 10.24   Bollinger bands.

intermediate-term trading, and 50 days for longer-term trading. These values typically apply to stocks and bonds, thus shorter time periods will be preferred by commodity traders. See Figure 10.24.

Bollinger bands require two trader-selected input variables: the number of days in the moving average index and the number of standard deviations to plot above and below the moving average. Over 95 percent of all the daily closes fall within three standard deviations from the mean of the time series. Typical values for the second parameter range from 1.5 to 2.5 standard deviations.

As with moving average envelopes, the basic interpretation of Bollinger bands is that prices tend to stay within the upper and lower band. The distinctive characteristic of Bollinger bands is that the spacing between the bands varies based on the volatility of the prices. During periods of extreme price changes (that is, high volatility), the bands widen to become more forgiving. During periods of stagnant pricing (that is, low volatility), the bands narrow to contain prices.

Bollinger notes the following characteristics of Bollinger bands:

- Sharp price changes tend to occur after the bands tighten, as volatility lessens.
- When prices move outside the bands, a continuation of the current trend is implied.
- Bottoms and tops made outside the bands followed by bottoms and tops made inside the bands call for reversals in the trend.

- A move that originates at one band tends to go all the way to the other band. This observation is useful when projecting price targets.

Bollinger bands do not generate buy and sell signals alone. They should be used with another indicator, usually the relative strength index. This is because when price touches one of the bands, it could indicate one of two things: a continuation of the trend or it could indicate a reaction the other way. So Bollinger bands used by themselves do not provide all of what technicians need to know, which is when to buy and sell. MACD can be used in conjunction with Bollinger bands and RSI.

Swing Analysis

Swing analysis is one of those nebulous terms that means different things to different people. It is often associated with swing trading, which also harbors a variety of connotations (the swing trader usually keeps a trade open longer than the typical session or day trader).

Within the framework of this book, we will define swing analysis as the study of the distance between local peaks and troughs in the closing prices for the purpose of identifying recurring patterns and correlations. The swing chart, like its older sibling the point and figure chart, requires the use of a massaging algorithm that filters out lateral congestion (whipsawing) during periods of low volatility. For this purpose, a minimum box size must be selected. Within currency trading, this is almost always a single pip in the quote (second) currency of the currency pair. Additionally, a minimum reversal quantity must be selected. This is simply the number of pips (box sizes) required before a retracement can be drawn in the opposite direction (the continuation of an existing trend requires only one box size to plot the next point).

Unlike the P&F chart, the swing chart does not distort the time element. That is, swing charts are frequently overlaid directly on top of a vertical bar chart since both use the same numerical scaling for the *x*- and the *y*-axis. See Figure 10.25.

In Figure 10.25, it is clear that a swing chart is a sequence of alternating straight lines, called waves, which connect each peak with its succeeding trough and vice versa.

The swing analyst is particularly interested in retracement percentages. Market behavior is such that when a major trend does break out, there is a sequence of impulse waves in the direction of the trend with interceding retracement waves (also called corrective waves). The ratio of the corrective wave divided by the preceding impulse wave is referred to as the percentage of retrace-

FIGURE 10.25   Bar chart with swing analysis overlay.

ment. Famous analysts such as William D. Gann and Ralph N. Elliott have dedicated their lives to interpreting these ratios and estimating the length of the next wave in the time series.

Gann believed that market waves moved in patterns based upon, among other things, the Fibonacci number series, which emphasizes the use of so-called magic numbers such as 38.2 percent, 50 percent, and 61.8 percent. Actually, there is no magic involved at all; they are simply proportions derived from the Golden Mean or Divine Ratio. This is a complete study unto itself and has many fascinating possibilities. Visit *http://www-groups.dcs.st-and.ac.uk/~history/Mathematicians/Fibonacci.html* for more details on Fibonacci and his work.

In his analysis of stocks in the 1920s and 1930s, Elliott was able to identify and categorize nine levels of cycles (that is, a sequence of successive waves) over the same time period for a single bar chart. This entailed increasing the minimum reversal threshold in the filtering algorithm, which creates fewer but longer waves with each new iteration. He believed each major impulse wave was composed of five smaller waves while major corrective waves were composed of only three smaller waves. We refer interested readers to the Web site *www.elliottwave.com* for more details on Elliott and his theories.

Advanced Studies

This chapter serves as a stepping stone into the realm of technical analysis. Time series analysis is a complex and ever-changing discipline. Advanced studies include deviation analysis, retracement studies, statistical regressions, Fibonacci progressions, Fourier transforms, and the Box-Jenkins method, to name just a few.

Into the Future

There are also those using techniques from other disciplines to analyze the markets. Michael Duane Archer, coauthor of this book, has deeply explored the use of Cellular Automata to forecast FOREX prices.

Your analysis of the markets is only *one* component of your trading system. In fact, two other components are more important, in the opinion of the authors: money management and psychology (discussed in detail in later chapters). Most traders who fail (and most traders do fail) tend to spend all their energies on developing a trading system at the expense of money management and trading psychology. *Don't be like them!*

The Technician's Creed

All market fundamentals are depicted in the actual market data. So the actual market fundamentals need not be studied in detail.

History repeats itself and therefore markets move in fairly predictable, or at least quantifiable, patterns. These patterns, generated by price movement, are called signals. The goal in technical analysis is to uncover the signals exhibited in a current market by examining past market signals.

Prices move in trends. Technicians typically do not believe that price fluctuations are random and unpredictable. Prices can move in one of three directions: up, down, or sideways. Once a trend in any of these directions is established, it usually will continue for some period. Trends occur at all price levels: tick, 5-minute, 1-hour, 1-day, weekly. What is a trend at the 1-minute level is obviously just a small blip on the radar on a weekly chart. Curiously, the various prices levels are interconnected.

Never make a trading decision based solely on a single indicator. The eclectic approach of comparing several indicators and charts at the same time is the best strategy.

As in all other aspects of trading, be very disciplined when using technical analysis. Too often, a trader fails to sell or buy into a market even after it has reached a price that his technical studies have identified as an entry or exit point. This is money management and psychology, not technical analysis, and both are *very* important!

Do you understand the differences between fundamental analysis and technical analysis?

The basic types of technical analysis tools are charts, moving averages, oscillators, and momentum analysis. In Chapter 12: Trading Tactics we will put forth a suggested program for developing your own technical analysis arsenal. Your analysis of the markets is only one of three components to successful trading—money management and psychology are the others.

Part

4

The Business of Trading

Chapter 11

Money Management and Psychology

The Trading Triangle

There are three components to a trading program: trading method, money management, and psychology or attitude. The vast majority of traders spend almost all of their efforts on a trading method. Yet most successful traders will tell you of the three, the trading method is the least important.

You do well by allocating significant thought and effort to the other two components. How much you weigh them determines your trading triangle. See Figure 11.1.

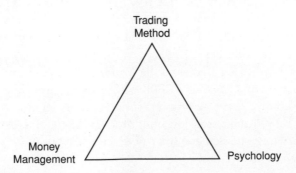

FIGURE 11.1   The trading triangle.

Money Management Factors

Money management is obviously about how you manage the money you trade; it includes both your trading capital and how you determine your exit from a trade, as in taking profits or setting stop-losses.

Most trading methods determine when you enter a trade, but not when you exit. If your trading method does automatically determine such factors, be careful the rules are not too restrictive. Most traders prefer something of a separate ad hoc method of determining trade exits.

Allocating your capital is a function of how large a percentage of trades you expect to be winners versus losers and the ratio between amount won and amount lost. The higher your percentage of winners and the greater the ratio between winners and losers, the less winning trades you need to make.

Be realistic. Do not expect to hit 80 percent winning trades with a 10:1 ratio between gains and losses. Position traders are happy to hit 30 percent of their trades, but expect a ratio of perhaps 5:1 on wins/losses. By contrast, guerilla scalpers figure a 1:1 ratio between winning dollars and losing dollars, so they need perhaps 60 percent winners to stay in the game. Consider your trading method and what type of trader you are, then construct trading triangles for 25 percent, 50 percent, and 100 percent annual returns.

Risk/Reward Ratio

One of the most crucial aspects of trading any security is the trader's propensity toward the ever-present risk factor. The risk/reward ratio is a nebulous, frequently underestimated component of trading that makes the trade possible. Without risk, there would be no profit or loss, just transaction costs.

Paradoxically, in the risk/reward ratio, the reward part is traditionally listed first. So a 4:1 ratio indicates that the reward is 4 times greater than the risk. Attempting to quantify the risk/reward ratio is a tricky endeavor. Let us assume that the trader has decided upon a 3:1 ratio and wants to initiate a long (buy) position in the EUR/USD currency pair based upon some recently acquired fundamental studies.

The current price is 1.2500 and the "fundamentals" indicate that there will be an upward rally to a price of 1.2800 within the next 36 hours (no rollover required). To "enforce" a risk/reward ratio of 3:1, our trader must set a take-profit limit order at 1.2800 and a stop-loss limit order at 1.2400. It is assumed that the trader has entered the market at a price of exactly 1.2500.

The math looks like this.

Take-profit spread: 1.2800 − 1.2500 = 300 pips
Stop-loss spread: 1.2500 − 1.2400 = 100 pips

Thus, the risk/reward ratio can be quantified as the quotient of the take-profit spread divided by the stop-loss spread.

Let us also assume our trader had sufficient equity in a margin account to execute the trade with a unit size of one lot (100k of Euros). The broker offers two percent margin trading (50:1 leverage). Each pip in a lot of the EUR/USD pair is worth USD 10.00. Thus, if the targeted price of 1.2800 is triggered first, the trader makes a profit of:

$$\text{USD } 10.00 \times 50{:}1 \text{ leverage} \times 300 \text{ pips} = \text{USD } 60{,}000$$

However, if the stop-loss limit is triggered first, the trader will lose:

$$\text{USD } 10.00 \times 50{:}1 \text{ leverage} \times 100 \text{ pips} = \text{USD } 20{,}000$$

The selection of a risk/reward ratio is highly subjective and is something that the trader must decide carefully after considering many factors including his or her trading style and trading methodology.

Ad Hoc Adjustment of Limit Orders

The notion of losing 20,000 dollars on one trade (as in the previous example) should make all traders cringe. However, the trader can limit his or her potential losses by "tightening the reins" of the trade, that is, moving both the take-profit and the stop-loss limit orders closer to the market entry price.

The trader can cut the loss potential to one-fourth the loss potential in the example by raising the stop-loss to 1.2475 and lowering the take-profit to 1.2600. If the price direction begins to react adversely, the trader may even elect to exit early by manually liquidating the trade.

However, if the price direction moves favorably, then the trader should raise both limit orders accordingly. At some point, he or she may even move the stop-loss limit order above the market entry price, thus "locking in" guaranteed profits. At the time, the trader still has the potential to hit the originally targeted price of 1.2800.

Early Liquidation

When dealing with long (buy) positions, the trader should hesitate lowering a stop-loss limit order. Accept the small loss and examine a different currency pair for market entry possibilities. A take-profit limit in a long position should only be lowered if the trader is fairly certain a period of lateral congestion or a reversal is about to occur. It may even be better to simply liquidate. The converse is true for short (sell) positions. But the road to large losses usually starts with moving or removing a stop-loss order!

If at any point the trader becomes overrun with uncertainty (a polite word for fear), doubt, and confusion, it is better to manually liquidate the trade with a small profit or loss than to hang on dismally waiting for a large loss.

More Ideas on Setting Stops

Don't put stops where everyone else does!

Stop-losses are typically placed below or above a previous low or high. We prefer to set stops as a function of market volatility. Look at some recent charts for the pairs you trade and the data and time frame you will use to actually execute a trade. Average the subtrends in the major trend direction and average the subtrends in the minor trend direction. Redo these averages occasionally to also get an idea of how volatility is shifting. Use the information to set price objectives and also stops. The technique may also be utilized for entry point purposes.

Trade Capital Allocation

Never allocate more than 10 percent of your trading capital to a single trade, either as margin or risk. Never start trading until you have funds for at least 30, and preferably 50 or more, trades.

Suppose your starting capital or grubstake is $3,000.00. Break it into three portions of $1,000.00 each. Then, break each of those down into 10 trades of $100 each. If you lose the first $1,000.00, take a deep breath and maybe a few days off. If you lose the second $1,000.00, spend some time analyzing your approach to the markets and making minor adjustments—resist the temptation to completely retool every time you have a bad trade or a losing streak.

Obviously you must consider your trading method and your trading type. You can be a scalper on small lots risking $50 a trade, but you cannot be a position trader on large lots with the same risk. Consider all factors in proportion.

Trade logical transaction sizes. Margin trading allows the FOREX trader a very large amount of leverage; trading at full margin capacity can make for some very large profits or losses on an account. Scaling your trades so that you may reenter the market or make transactions on other currencies is generally wiser. In short, do not trade amounts that can potentially wipe you out and do not put all your eggs in one basket. See Figure 11.2.

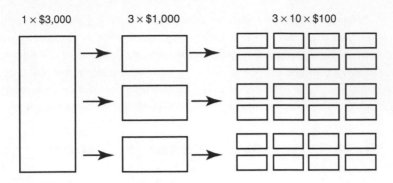

FIGURE 11.2 Sample allocation program.

Stick with your trading method long enough to give it a chance to work. Don't even make your first trade until you have studied it under different market environments. This applies to your money management plan too: Give it an opportunity to work.

Trading Psychology

Trading psychology is what separates the men from the boys, the women from the girls. You might have made a small mint through paper-trading, but when real money is on the line "things" happen. Know thyself!

Fear and Greed, Greed and Fear!

By nature all people are emotionally attached to their money. Since the you will be trading with funds that you have already defined as nonessential to your well being, you must cultivate an attitude of emotional detachment from your FOREX trading account. This is emotional detachment—not indifference or nonchalance. Otherwise, each sour trade will infest you with stress, worry, and fear. Currency trading is not worth an ulcer.

On the other side of the coin is overconfidence. One very profitable trade can induce the novice trader to go "gung-ho" and trade more currency pairs than he or she can track efficiently in one trading session. Overconfidence tends to breed avarice and avarice can lead to financial shakiness. Moderation, level-headedness, experience, and intuition all play key roles in the formula to successful currency trading. Knowing when to take a calculated risk definitely helps, too.

To paraphrase pioneer technical analyst J. Welles Wilder in his book *The Adam Theory of Markets*: The first idea is one of emotion and attitude, namely that in order to be successful one must "surrender" to the market. If one ceases to worry about what might happen or what should happen, then one is free to concentrate on what the market is doing, which is where the profit will be made.

Characteristics of Successful Traders

There are some very basic characteristics attributed to most successful traders whether they are in stocks, bonds, futures, or currencies:

- Successful traders tend to have absolute control over their emotions—they never get too elated over a win or too depressed over a loss.
- Successful traders seldom think of prices as "too high" or "too low."
- Successful traders do not panic—they make evolutionary adjustments rather than revolutionary changes to their trading style.
- Successful traders do not flinch at making the decision to take a loss, never let losses ride, and never add to losing trades.

    One old trader told me he thought of his positions as stock in a retail store. If something sells and is making you money, you add to that line. If something is not selling and costing you money, you discount it and unload it as quickly as possible.

- Successful traders treat trading as business and not a hobby.
- Successful traders stay physically fit.
- Successful traders are prepared for all eventualities on any given trading day. They come to work with a plan that includes many contingencies and not just what they hope will happen.

    In your own trading program you should have predetermined answers to the following questions: What happens if...

- prices open sharply higher or lower?
- the market is very quiet?
- the market is very volatile?
- the market makes new highs?
- the market makes new lows?
- the market goes up early and reverses later?
- the market goes down early and reverses later?

- The successful trader trades only with money he or she can afford to lose.

   Trading FOREX is speculative and can result in substantial losses. It is also exciting, exhilarating, and can be addictive. The more you are emotionally involved with your money, the harder it is to make objective, clear-headed decisions about market entry and exit.

- Successful traders spend at least as much time focusing on money management as they do on a trading method.

   You don't have the profile of a successful trader if at least some of the above traits don't sound like you. We will offer a few additional money management and psychology guidelines in later chapters.

- Successful traders keep a low profile.

- Successful traders "listen" to the markets. Unsuccessful traders attempt to impose their will on the market.

12

Trading Tactics

This chapter is a potpourri of topics that collectively will determine your trading style. Style is what criteria you use to make selections in various areas of trading. A trading style does not develop out of the blue but will emerge as you make your first trades. But now is a good time to begin thinking about these intangibles. Once you start trading, continue to think about your trading style from time to time. Giving yourself feedback on an ongoing basis is the best way to stay fresh and avoid getting in a rut or just plain going nuts from watching the markets.

Trading Strategy

Trading successfully is by no means a simple matter. It requires time, market knowledge, market understanding, and a large amount of self-restraint. Anyone who says you can consistently make money in foreign exchange markets is being untruthful. Foreign exchange is by nature a volatile market. The practice of trading it by way of margin increases that volatility geometrically.

We are therefore talking about a very fast market that is naturally inconsistent. Following that precept, it is logical to say that in order to make a successful trade, a trader has to take into account technical and fundamental data and make an informed decision based on his or her perception of market sentiment and market expectation. Timing a trade correctly is probably the most important aspect of trading successfully, but invariably there will be cases where a trader's timing is off. A successful trader does not expect to generate returns on every trade.

Let's examine what a trader needs to do in order to increase his or her chances for profitable trades.

Trade with Money You Can Afford to Lose

Trading FOREX markets is speculative and can result in losses. It is also exciting, exhilarating, and can be addictive. The more you are involved with your money, the harder it is to make a clear-headed decision. Money you have earned is precious, but money you need for survival should never be traded.

Identify the State of the Market

What is the market doing? Is it trending upwards or downwards? Is it in a trading range? Is the trend strong or weak? Did it begin long ago or does it look like a new trend is forming? Getting a clear picture of the market situation is laying the groundwork for a successful trade. No matter how complex and leading-edge your trading system might be, it never hurts to sit back and eyeball the charts. Markets often have a remarkable rhythm. Look for the following:

- The length of the primary trend versus the secondary trend.
- The average time between tops and bottoms.
- The average range of a bar, whether you are watching 1-minute, 5-minute, hourly, or daily data.

You will see different rhythms for the same market when viewing charts at different scales—for example, 1-minute, 1-hour, and daily. Put these rhythms together for a true perspective on things.

Identify the Market Environment

Every market may be defined on a continuum of *price movement,* or trend slope, and *volatility.* Volatility measures how much prices move in the aggregate over some fixed period of time. Figure 12.1 indicates an arbitrary scale of 1 to 8 for purposes of example only. This can also be studied on different chart-time matrices.

All markets may be measured as an index of where they reside on both these lines. For example, a market with a very high trend slope and low volatility could be represented as a "7-2" market.

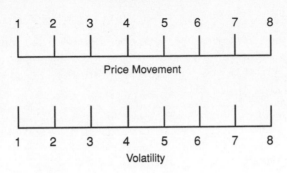

FIGURE 12.1 Price movement and volatility.

Price movement is the defined slope of a trend from beginning to end point. See Figure 12.2.

Volatility is the total amount of price movement over a specified time. See Figure 12.3.

In technical analysis we discussed the concept of trading environment—that all market activity can be defined by where it sits on two scales of volatility and price movement. Keep the market environment in mind and watch for both evolutionary and revolutionary shifts. The elements of the trading environment are the time frame and the three-chart system.

Time Frame Many traders get in the market without thinking when they would like to get out—after all, the goal is to make money. When trading, the trader must extrapolate the movement that he or she expects to happen. Within this extrapolation resides a price evolution during a certain period of time.

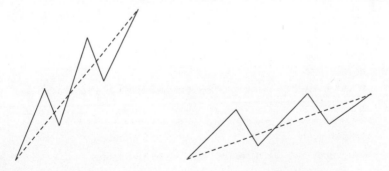

FIGURE 12.2 Price movement.

FIGURE 12.3 Volatility.

Attached to this is the idea of exit price. The importance of this is to mentally put your trade in perspective. Although it is clearly impossible to know exactly when you will exit the market, it is important to define from the outset if you will be "scalping" (trying to get a few points off the market), trading intraday, or trading over a longer term.

This will also determine what chart period you are examining. If you trade many times a day, there is no point basing your technical analysis on a daily graph: You will instead want to analyze 30-minute or hourly graphs. It is also important to know the different time periods when various financial centers enter and exit the market, as this creates more or less volatility and liquidity and can influence market movements.

The Three-Chart System Determine your desired trading time frame. If, for example, you use hourly charts to determine entry and exit, then use 5-minute charts for detail and daily charts for a long view of things. If you use 5-minute charts to trade, use 1-minute charts for detail and hourly ones for the long view. See also Table 12.1 for more on timing matrices.

TABLE 12.1	Timing Matrices for Different Traders		
Trader	*Timing*	*Home*	*Trend*
Scalper	Tick	1 to 5 Minutes	1 Hour
Day Trader	1 Minute	5 to 10 Minutes	1 Day
Position Trader	10 Minutes	1 to 24 Hours	2 Days

Time Your Trade

You can be right about a potential market movement but be too early or too late when you enter the trade. Timing considerations are twofold: An expected market figure like the consumer price index, retail sales, or a federal reserve decision can consolidate a movement that is already underway. Timing your move means knowing what is expected and taking into account all considerations before trading. Technical analysis can help you identify when and at what price a move may occur. We will look at technical analysis in more detail later.

If In Doubt, Stay Out

The conservative Belgian dentist strategy is "Sit on your hands, sit on your hands." The bulls make money, the bears make money, but the pigs just get slaughtered! (The bulls prefer advancing markets, the bears trade in declining markets, while the pigs expect quick killings in any market.)

Trade Logical Transaction Sizes

Margin trading allows the FOREX trader a very large amount of leverage, but trading at full margin capacity can make for some very large profits or losses on an account. Scaling your trades so that you may reenter the market or make transactions on other currencies is generally wiser. In short, do not trade amounts that can potentially wipe you out and do not put all your eggs in one basket.

Gauge Market Sentiment

Market sentiment is what most of the market is perceived to be feeling about the market and therefore what it is doing or will do. This is essentially about trend. You may have heard the phrase "the trend is your friend," which means that if you are in the right direction with a strong trend you will make successful trades. This of course is very simplistic; a trend is capable of reversal at any time. Technical and fundamental data can indicate, however, if the trend began long ago and if it is strong or weak.

Exercise Contrary Opinion

Never be afraid to go against the crowd—the crowd is almost always wrong. Follow the old Wall Street adage "Buy the rumor, sell the news."

Know the Market Expectation

Market expectation relates to what most people are expecting as far as upcoming news is concerned. If people are expecting an interest rate to rise and it does, then there usually will not be much of a movement because the information will already have been "discounted" by the market; alternatively, if the adverse happens, markets will usually react violently.

Watch what other traders are doing but don't follow them!

In a perfect world, every trader would be looking at a 14-day RSI (Relative Strength Indicator) and making trading decisions based on that. If that were the case, when RSI would go under the 30 percent level, everyone would buy and by consequence the price would rise. Needless to say, the world is not perfect and not all market participants follow the same technical indicators, draw the same trend lines, or identify the same support and resistance levels.

The great diversity of opinions and techniques used translates directly into price diversity. Traders, however, have a tendency to use a limited variety of technical tools. The most common are 9- and 14-day RSI, obvious trend lines and support levels, Fibonacci retracement, MACD, and 9-, 20- and 40-day exponential moving averages. The closer you get to what most traders are looking at, the more precise your estimations will be. The reason for this is simple arithmetic: Larger numbers of buyers than sellers at a certain price will move the market up from that price and vice versa.

Check the various FOREX discussion groups once a week to see how the majority of traders perceive the market. Just don't be a slave to the news.

Trading Tactics

This section concerns the actual details on trade execution, tracking, and exiting. It also assumes that every trading session is attended (that is, that the trader is monitoring the price action while in motion and does not walk away from his or her trading platform).

Once the trader has selected the currency pair, the position to take (buy or sell), and the number of units to trade, he or she will initiate the trade.

The trader has two options for entering into a new trade. The simplest is either a market order in which the trade is executed at the current market price or a limit order in which the order is delayed until the market price hits the limit order price that the trader specified.

At the same time that the trader enters the market, he or she must also set both of the stop-loss and take-profit limit moves. As mentioned earlier, by trading without a stop-loss safeguard, you are unnecessarily exposing yourself to tremendous risk that can clear out part or all of your margin.

Setting a reasonable take-profit limit is also important in the event there is a power glitch or some other disrupting anomaly. Modern computers are taking longer to reboot, after which you must log into your broker's trading platform. In the four to eight minutes that the restarting process requires, an open trade may have hit a respectable level of profit return, but the realization did not occur because you did not place a take-profit limit order or you set it too far from the entry price.

The placement of the stop-loss and take-profit limits is highly subjective and is based on the trader's sensitivity to risk. Several trading platforms automatically calculate these values (stop-loss and take-profit) when you click on a check box. Their calculation algorithm may be a simple linear distance from the entry price (say, 15, 20, or 25 pips in both directions) or it may involve some percentage of the current range of trading. Either way, you are at liberty to adjust the stop-loss and take-profit limit orders in an open position.

In a position that moves against you, it is recommended that the trader let the price action trigger the liquidation of the order and simply absorb the loss. Or, if you believe that the price direction will not reverse itself in your favor, you may liquidate the position manually before the stop-loss is triggered. It is not recommended that you lower the stop-loss in a long position with the hopes that the price will reverse shortly and move in the opposite direction. The odds are against it. Take the loss, stand up, walk around, clear your head, and start over, preferably by examining a different currency pair.

This is the disappointing part to trading. However, when prices move in your favor, you have more options based on price volatility. If the price moves significantly in your favor (say, 15 to 20 pips in a buy position), then move the stop-loss above the entry price (say, three to five pips) and raise the take-profit limit order by 20 pips or so. As the trade continues to advance favorably, continue raising both the stop-loss and the take-profit orders.

In this manner, you can successfully "lock in" guaranteed profits while letting the market run its course. Large profits can be realized using this mechanism. The exit mechanism should not be triggered by hitting the take-profit limit but by a reversal, triggering the favorably adjusted stop-loss limit order. The exception is when you "feel" it is time and exit manually.

However, the subjective part is how closely the two limit orders should be set in relation to the current price. When setting the initial values for both the stop-loss and take-profit orders, look for support and resistance lines in the prices immediately preceding the current price. This will give you some idea of the range of trading in the immediate past.

Lastly, we should discuss pyramiding. This trading tactic involves adding to a favorable open position. This is done very simply by initiating new orders in the same currency pair and in the same position (buy or sell). This tactic may be handled profitably by veteran traders but is not recommended for the novice trader. The trader must be ever-conscious of margin requirements and the amount remaining in his or her account. Using unrealized profits as the margin for new trades has landed many a trader in deep trouble. Sharp market reversals in pyramid trading have a devastating effect on the trader's margin account. Be forewarned!

Eclectic Approach

Should you use fundamental analysis or technical analysis to determine the details of my trades? The veteran technician will adamantly respond "technical analysis" while the fundamentalist will confidently reply "fundamental analysis."

The correct answer is both. Any current market data deemed valid, whether fundamental or technical, should never be ignored. It is, however, a very subjective decision on the part of the trader; how much "weight" to put on either discipline is learned from experience. Do not be afraid to change your trading methodology from time to time. But keep changes evolutionary, not revolutionary. Do not make changes just because a single trade went sour.

Selecting Markets to Trade

We recommend that the novice trader begin by trading the major USD currency pairs only. These pairs usually require a lower bid/ask pip spread, which increases your profit potential while reducing your transaction costs.

In addition to the transaction costs, you must also examine the current volatility of each candidate currency pair. Statistically, volatility is usually defined as the standard deviation of a data sample. However, this is a somewhat laborious process since it entails summing all the elements in the data sample. In Table 12.2 we use the lazy man's method for calculating two relatives of volatility, called the absolute range and the relative range of the data sample.

Absolute range is converted from a decimal value to number of pips by multiplying by 1,000 (or 10 in some cases) and expressed as pips in the quote (second) currency.

TABLE 12.2   Calculating Absolute and Relative Range

midrange   = (high + low) /2

absolute range = high − low

relative range = 100 × range / midrange

The time period used in Table 12.3 is July 1, 2003, through December 31, 2003. The table is divided into three groups: USD major currency pairs, USD minors, and non-USD cross pairs.

Currency pairs with a relative range value less than 1.50 should probably be avoided due to lack of volatility, unless the trader knows how to profit from horizontal markets (this involves scalping small profits from numerous trades and accrues a very large transaction cost in the account summary). Even though Table 12.3 required several thousand ticks to compile, it is in no way conclusive.

Absolute range is a statistic that characterizes an important property of a single currency pair. Relative range is used to compare multiple currency pairs with each other.

TABLE 12.3		Selecting Currency Pair Criteria			
Currency Pair	6-Month High	6-Month Low	Adjusted Range	Relative Range	Bid/Ask Spread
EUR/USD	1.2542	1.0796	1746	3.74	3
USD/JPY	120.36	106.92	1344	3.05	3
GBP/USD	1.8106	1.5663	2443	3.62	3
USD/CHF	1.4217	1.2434	1783	3.35	3
USD/CAD	1.4079	1.2834	1245	2.31	4
AUD/USD	0.7662	0.6355	1307	4.66	4
NZD/USD	0.6839	0.5643	1196	4.79	5
USD/SGD	1.7645	1.7008	637	0.92	8
USD/HKD	7.8104	7.7089	1015	0.33	10
USD/DKK	6.8898	5.9401	9497	3.70	35
USD/MXN	11.4319	10.7456	6863	1.55	50
USD/ZAR	3.7942	3.7513	429	0.28	90
EUR/JPY	137.31	124.84	1247	2.38	3
EUR/GBP	0.7113	0.6812	301	1.08	3
EUR/CHF	1.5749	1.5322	427	0.69	3
CHF/JPY	89.24	79.29	995	2.95	6
GBP/JPY	194.76	180.15	1461	1.95	9
EUR/AUD	1.7567	1.6048	1519	2.26	12
EUR/CZK	32.9606	31.4485	15121	1.17	60

Selecting Trading Parameters

Once you have selected the trading currency pair and determined a market entry price, you must decide the remaining parameters:

Trade Unit Size

This only applies if the broker allows the trader to deal in odd-lot sizes. One recommendation for small-capital traders is that no single trade should ever exceed 10 percent of the trader's margin account.

Stop-Loss Order Differential

This differential defines the number of pips below the entry price that the stop-loss limit order is placed in a buy (long) trade and vice versa in a sell (short) trade.

Take-Profit Order Differential

This differential defines the number of pips above the entry price that the take-profit limit order is placed in a buy (long) trade and vice versa in a sell (short) trade.

You need to be realistic about these numbers and willing to make adjustments along the way. It is not reasonable to have a 10-pip stop-loss order and a 500-pip take-profit order. Scale your differentials to the type of trading you are doing and the ratio you reasonably expect between winning trades and losing trades. For example, when trading the EUR/USD pair, you might initialize the market entry trade with a 15-pip stop-loss and a 30-pip take-profit order.

Duration

Duration, or expiry, is used on limit orders only and denotes the length of time that you want the broker to keep an untriggered limit order active. We recommend keeping all limit orders to less than a day (or even a few hours). The logic here is that while trading in a different currency pair, the limit order on the first currency pair may trigger, thereby reducing the amount of available margin.

Trading Matrices

Market action is constantly occurring at different levels, or price matrices, concurrently. A price matrix consists of three consecutive "legs" in a price action: an initial trend either up or down, a retracement movement in the opposite direction, and a final leg in the same direction as the first leg (see Figure 12.4).

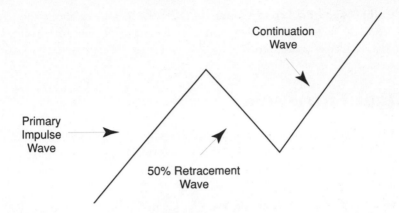

FIGURE 12.4   Basic upward price matrix.

We typically measure these based on the time interval involved: streaming tick data, 1-minute data, 5-minute data, hourly data, daily data, and weekly data. Specifically, parameters must be set to determine when to draw the retracement leg. Typically, either a minimum percentage of the preceding leg must occur or a minimum number of pips in the opposite direction will "trigger" a new leg as shown in Figure 12.5.

An important decision to make early on is: At what level am I trading, primarily? Types of traders are related to the matrix level they call "home." Scalpers are most associated with tick data, day traders with 1-minute and 5-minute data, and position traders with hourly data. Because of the volatility and leverage in the FOREX markets, few traders call daily data home.

While you want to call one or two neighboring levels home, it is a mistake to avoid giving attention to the levels below and above your home. Typically you

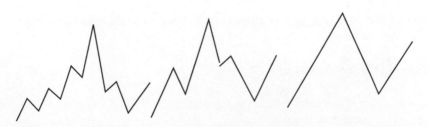

FIGURE 12.5   Trading matrices with different minimum triggering mechanisms.

want to follow the market with your home levels; get ideas about the overall trend from the matrix just above, and use the matrix below for timing your entry, exit, and stop-loss orders.

Dagger Entry Rule

The Dagger Entry Rule was first published by Mike Archer in *Denver Magazine* in June 1978. It is used to determine the price level for an efficient market entry point and consists of three steps:

> Step 1: We wait for a major trend to form. Call it (A). Step 2: We watch for a price correction in the opposite direction; call it (B). The third step is to complete the dagger: Wait for a sign of an end to the down trend (B) and buy as soon as prices start up again. The dagger, of which I have given only the basics, guarantees that you buy at bargain levels and also that you do not attempt to pick the bottom of the market.

See Figure 12.6.

Market Timing

Here are some tips for getting the most of market timing. When developing your own personalized FOREX trading strategy, there are many factors you can

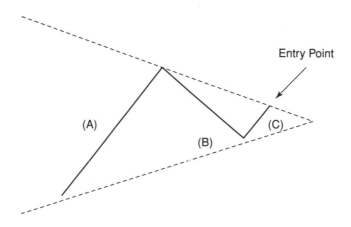

FIGURE 12.6   The dagger entry rule.

research that can turn to your advantage. Four of these involve timing: market opening, market closing, time of day, and day of week.

Market Opening

Officially the FOREX market opens at 5:30 PM ET, though different brokers react differently in different time zones. Keep in mind that over the weekend all currency pairs carry an extra premium in transaction costs. A normal 3-pip bid/ask spread during normal trading hours may increase to a 10-pip spread on weekends.

Once the weekend transaction costs return to normal, many pairs exhibit high volatility due to economic influences that occurred over the weekend. Analyzing a set number of currency pairs enhances your profit opportunities. Frequently a trend emerges in one direction or the other and continues until the weekend influences have been satisfied. This may entail tracking several pairs until the early hours of Monday morning. When opportunity knocks...

Market Closing

Many corporations like to clear out last-minute orders Friday afternoon to avoid possible rollover charges and to reduce the risk of any adverse anomalies that may occur over the weekend. This equates to increased volatility right before the market closes at 4:30 PM Friday afternoon.

If you trade during this peak period of volatility, always be certain to liquidate your trades before the bid/ask spread jumps to its increased weekend range.

Time of Day

For the most past, the highest volatility periods revolve around banking hours in New York City. This overlaps only slightly with banking hours in London and Frankfurt. Another factor is the time zone in which your broker is located. Taking these three factors into consideration plus your own time zone, you should be able to determine periods of high volatility that increase profit potential. See Appendix C for details on time zones and world banking hours.

Day of Week

The days on which the market opens and closes have already been discussed. Other days of the week may also have special significance. For instance, new interest rates are normally published on Thursdays, which causes immediate changes in USD currency pairs.

Summary

- The decisions you make about specific trading options—both strategy and tactics—determine your trading style. Be aware of your style, monitor it, and make changes wisely.

- Stop-loss and take-profit levels should be realistic and complementary to the type of trading you do.

- The market operates at many different levels or matrices concurrently. Identify your home levels early on in your career.

- Use matrices above and below your home for clues to the long-term trend and entry/exit points.

- When in doubt, *stay out!*

- The markets will always be around. Missing a potential opportunity is infinitely better than taking an actual loss.

What to Do
If Things Go Wrong

Evaluating Your Performance

We recommend that the novice trader start the trading experience with a simple handwritten log of his or her trades. This does not mean logging every single trade, which would be too cumbersome. Instead, record a simple synopsis of each day's performance similar to the format shown in Figure 13.1.

Trading Date	Beginning Balance	No. of Trades	Pairs Traded	Strategies Used	Ending Balance	Comment
7/1/2004						
7/2/2004						
7/3/2004						
7/4/2004						
7/5/2004						

FIGURE 13.1 Daily performance log.

Common Trading Mistakes

Throughout this book, we have mentioned several trading caveats and wish to resummarize them here (with others):

- **Trading without a stop-loss limit order.** Neglecting to set a stop loss is asking for financial disaster. In the event of a power outage, you may receive a margin call in the time it takes to reboot your computer.

- **Trading without a take-profit limit order.** Always set a reasonable take-profit limit order. Again, in the event of a power outage, the market may hit your expectations and reverse to the market entry price (or further) in the time it takes to reboot the computer. Always remember: When a trade is beginning to move favorably, you can adjust your take-profit farther from the market entry price.

- **Using too much of your margin.** Your margin requirement is recalculated with each price change. This is especially noticeable when you have sold a position and the price is advancing. For small-capital traders, we recommend never using more than one-third of the total account balance on any single trade.

- **Trading too many pairs at one time.** First, this could cause a margin call. Many dealers will liquidate all open trades if any single trade generates a margin call, which could potentially eradicate any profit. Second, it clutters up the screen (and the trader's attention) when five or more bar charts are displayed simultaneously on the screen.

- **Trading at the broker's closing time.** At closing time, most dealers increase the bid/ask spread to cover low volatility and liquidity. A 3-pip spread may jump to a 10-pip spread instantly, wiping out seven pips of hard-earned profit. Always check the broker's hours of operation and at what time the increased spread goes into effect.

- **Trading very obscure cross rates.** Trading non-USD cross currency pairs like HUF (the Hungarian forint) or SAR (the Saudi riyal) is not advisable. The bid/ask spread is abnormally high and volatility may be unusually low. Without volatility, your open trade could lapse into a rollover position (usually two days). This is best left to the professionals who may be using an obscure cross rate as a leg in triangular arbitrage trade.

- **Overconfidence.** "Pride goeth before destruction, and a haughty spirit before a fall." Try to keep everything in the proper perspective.

- **False expectations.** Currency trading offers no guarantees. Do not become discouraged over losses. After all, you are not risking monies earmarked as your survival fund.

- **Trading without a plan.** Never enter a trade without first examining the big picture. Most trading platforms allow the trader to view multiple time intervals of the same currency pair. Scrutinizing the 5-second chart alone is usually not sufficient. Also check the 1-minute chart, the 1-hour chart, and the 1-day chart, or whatever multiples the platform provides. A long-term trend may be in motion, which is not clearly visible in a short time interval chart. Also, any available technical and/or fundamental analysis on the targeted currency pair is also beneficial.

- **Never add to a losing position.** Exit the losing position, take a break, and start over. Compounding your loss will not force a price reversal.

- **Don't exit because of whipsawing.** When a market begins whipsawing near your market entry price, there is no urgency to liquidate the position. A fellow trader once commented, "Monitoring extended periods of whipsawing is like watching paint dry." We explained that the market is simply building up energy to make a significant breakout. In fact, most technicians feel that whatever price direction was in motion prior to whipsawing will resume in that same direction after the whipsawing period. Patience is a trading quality that must be learned.

- **Lack of focus.** Pay very close attention when initiating a new order. The two most common mistakes are entering the wrong action (buy or sell) and mistyping the number of units to trade. Neither can be corrected once the entry order is executed except by liquidation.

- **Clouded judgment.** Never let the results of a sour trade affect your judgment criteria for the subsequent trade. Each trade is a separate entity. Simply reversing the market action (buy to sell or sell to buy) after a loss does not guarantee that the current trend will continue.

- **If in doubt, don't trade.** This speaks for itself. It is always better to make no trades than a series of costly trades. Take the day off or at least wait an hour or two.

Correcting Errors

The following guidelines should be reviewed even when things are moving smoothly:

- First, take a break. The markets will be there an hour from now.
- Review your performance log in detail. Pinpoint your strengths and your weaknesses.
- Reread Chapter 12, "Trading Tactics." It may be time to adjust your approach to the market.

- You may need to increase or decrease the number of pips that you are using to set the stop-loss and take-profit limit orders.

- Determine if you are entering the market too early or too late. Proper market timing is the key to profitable trading.

- You may want to lower the number of units traded (temporarily) simply to rebolster trading confidence.

- Try trading at different times in the day even if it means getting up early. Also, there is no reason that you cannot trade any of the seven major USD currencies pairs or even the cross rates with the EUR, JPY, and GBP currencies once you gain some trading experience.

- Nearly all FOREX trading platforms will provide an Activity Log that itemizes the details of each trade. Display the log on the screen (or even print a hard copy) to scrutinize any shortcomings on your part.

When to Say "Uncle"

It may be wise to set a threshold percentage of the original equity that you deposited with your broker. If your current balance drops below this threshold level, you may need to reevaluate your priorities. A change in attitude or greater flexibility may be indicated. As we mentioned earlier, currency trading may not suit everyone's disposition.

14

Record Keeping

Edge Financial Company, Inc.
9730 SW Cascade Blvd., #200
Tigard, OR 97223-4324

W e find it useful to keep daily and weekly records of our trading plans, thoughts, and activities. It's important to come to the markets well prepared for many contingencies. The records will also help you diagnose problems and find solutions.

Daily Trade Plan and Evaluation

In the previous chapter, we recommended that novice traders maintain a simple handwritten daily performance sheet and an account balance sheet. By scrutinizing this data at the end of the trading session, traders will be able to identify their strengths and weaknesses and develop a "feel" for market characteristics for different currency pairs, trading times, and chart patterns.

Weekly Trade Plan and Evaluation

Here is a suggested weekly trade plan and evaluation:

- *Plans* should include decision contingencies for various market actions for that trading session; this is very similar to football coaches' "scripting" the first few plays of a game.

- *Evaluations* should include what went right and what went wrong, as well as a brief text summary of the session.

You may add more to your daily and weekly summaries based on your specific trading program.

Novice traders may review their daily performance and account balance sheets collectively to ascertain any weaknesses in the trading system. Scanning the daily sheets for wins and losses helps put the entire endeavor in proper perspective. Adding comments and ideas to the weekly plan provides insight when reviewed later and assists traders in recognizing the direction of their market acumen and development.

The Tax Man

Regrettably, profits and losses from FOREX trades in the United States are subject to short-term (one year or less) capital gains tax as dictated by the Internal Revenue Service. The governments of other civilized countries will also be happy to share in any good fortune that might come your way in the markets.

The basic U.S. reporting instrument is Form 1040 Schedule D, though supplementary forms may also be required. Forms and instructions can be downloaded in portable document format (PDF) at *http://www.irs.gov/pub/*.

Consult your accountant for full details on taxes and the expensing of write-offs that you might be able to take for your trading activities.

Part 5

Advanced Topics

15

Advanced Topics

This chapter is optional for the novice trader though investors with some trading experience will find it informative.

Rollovers

A rollover is the process whereby the settlement of an open trade is rolled forward to another value date. The cost of this process is based on the interest rate differential of the two currencies.

In the spot FOREX market, trades must be settled within two business days. For example, if a trader sells a certain number of currency units on Wednesday, he or she must deliver an equivalent number of units on Friday. Yet currency trading systems may allow for a rollover, with which open positions can be swapped forward to the next settlement date (giving an extension of two additional business day). The interest rate for such a swap is predetermined, and, in fact, these swaps are actually financial instruments that can also be traded on the currency market.

In any spot rollover transaction the difference between the interest rates of the base and quote currencies is reflected as an overnight loan. If the trader holds a long position in the currency with the higher interest rate, he or she would gain on the spot rollover. The amount of such a gain would fluctuate day to day according to the precise interest rate differential between the base and the quote currency. Such rollover rates are quoted in dollars and are shown in the interest column of the FOREX trading system. Rollovers, however, will not affect traders who never hold a position overnight, since the rollover is exclusively a day-to-day phenomenon.

Some brokers will automatically roll over open trades while others may liquidate orders that exceed the two-day limitation. Also, some dealers may append a rollover charge in addition to the interest differential. Rollover credits or debits are reflected in the unrealized profit and loss column of the open position.

If you intend to maintain open positions longer than two days, carefully read your dealer's policy agreement or consult their customer service department. Also note that rollover costs may affect margin requirements.

Hedging

A hedge is a position or combination of positions in one security that reduces the risk of your primary position in the same security.

An example of hedging in commodity futures is the Midwest farmer who grows #1 Soft Red Wheat and intends to physically take his harvest to market for September delivery. After tilling the soil and planting the seeds in late spring, the farmer initiates a short (sell) commodity futures contract for September wheat at the Chicago Board of Trade at what he feels is a fair price. If the price of wheat declines dramatically in September, the farmer will suffer losses on his physical delivery but will make profits on his futures contract. If the price of wheat rises substantially in the fall, the farmer will make profits on his physical delivery but will suffer losses on his futures contract. Thus, hedging not only reduces risk but can also be used to lock in predetermined profits in some situations.

Normally when you have an open position to buy or sell at your FOREX dealer and you open a new position in the opposite direction, the two positions will close each other out. If you had a position for USD/CHF to buy, for example, and you opened a new position USD/CHF to sell, both positions would close, since you cannot buy and sell currencies at the same time. The feature of hedging, however, allows you to do exactly that if your FOREX dealer offers this trading feature.

When you open a hedge position, both positions (the original and the newly hedged one) will remain opened. You will have two positions, going in the opposite direction of each other in the same currency pair. This is used to lock your current loss or win, until you have a better understanding of where the market is moving. Theoretically, profit is to be gained by skillful timing of the liquidation orders. If liquidated at the same time, the trader will automatically lose only the transaction cost since the gain in one trade will be canceled exactly by the loss in the other trade.

Brokers who offer hedging do not normally require additional margin for the second hedged position. Consult your broker for details before attempting to apply this rather esoteric trading strategy.

Options Trading

An option is an agreement that gives the holder the option to buy or sell a specific security at a certain price within a certain time. Two types of options exist: call and put. A call is the right to buy while a put is the right to sell. One can write or buy call and put options.

Options on the foreign exchange are really no different from options on stock shares, commodity futures, or real estate. The basic premise is that the buyer of an option has the right but not the obligation to enter into a contract with the seller. Naturally the option owner exercises this right when it is to his or her advantage. Currency options specify a foreign exchange contract and give the owner the right to enter into the specified contract during a pre-agreed period of time.

FOREX options have gained acceptance as invaluable tools in managing foreign exchange risk. They are used extensively and make up between 5 and 10 percent of total volume of trading. Currency options bring a much wider range of hedging alternatives to portfolio managers and corporate treasuries.

An American option may be exercised at any valid business date throughout the life of the option, while a European option can only be exercised on the expiration date.

An option is said to have intrinsic value when the strike price of the option is more favorable than the current market forward rate. As a general rule, the greater the intrinsic value of an option, the higher its premium:

- An option with some intrinsic value is described as being "in-the-money."
- An option with no intrinsic value is said to be "out-of-the-money."
- Where the strike price of the option is equal to the current forward rate the option is said to be "at-the-money."

Consult your broker for details and margin requirements. Be particularly aware when dealing with options—it's an area that has attracted a substantial portion of the FOREX fraud.

Arbitrage

In general, arbitrage is the purchase or sale of any financial instrument and simultaneous taking of an equal and opposite position in a related market, in order to take advantage of small price differentials between markets. Essentially, arbitrage opportunities arise when currency prices go out of sync with each other. There are numerous forms of arbitrage involving multiple markets, future deliveries, options, and other complex derivatives. A less sophisticated example of a two-currency, two-location arbitrage transaction follows:

> Bank ABC offers 170 Japanese yen for one U.S. dollar and Bank XYZ offers only 150 yen for one dollar. Go to Bank ABC and purchase 170 yen. Next go to Bank XYZ and sell the yen for $1.13. In a little more than the time it took to cross the street that separates the two banks, you earned a 13 percent return on your original investment. If the anomaly between the two banks' exchange rates persists, repeat the transactions. After exchanging currencies at both banks six times, you will have more than doubled your investment.

Within the FOREX market, triangular arbitrage is a specific trading strategy that involves three currencies, their correlation, and any discrepancy in their parity rates. Thus, there are no arbitrage opportunities when dealing with just two currencies in a single market. Their fluctuations are simply the trading range of their exchange rate.

In the subsequent examples, we refer to the following tables of currency pairs consisting of the five most frequently traded pairs (USD, EUR, JPY, GBP, and CHF) with recent bid/ask rates. See Table 15.1.

We omitted the other two majors, CAD and AUD, for the sake of simplicity and not because there is a lack of arbitrage opportunities in these two majors.

Example 1

Two USD pairs and one cross pair (multiply)   First we must identify certain characteristics and distinguish the following categories:

- USD is the base currency (leftmost currency in the pair):

USD/CHF	1.2402/05
USD/JPY	105.61/64

- USD is the quote currency (rightmost currency in the pair):

EUR/USD	1.2638/40
GBP/USD	1.8275/78

TABLE 15.1 Combinations of the Five Most Frequently Traded Currencies			
Currency	Bid	Ask	Pip Spread
CHF/JPY	0.8514	0.8519	4
EUR/CHF	1.5676	1.5678	2
EUR/GBP	0.6915	0.6917	2
EUR/JPY	133.51	133.54	3
EUR/USD	1.2638	1.2640	2
GBP/CHF	2.2666	2.6674	8
GBP/JPY	193.02	193.10	8
GBP/USD	1.8275	1.8278	3
USD/CHF	1.2402	1.2405	3
USD/JPY	105.61	105.64	3

- Cross rates (non-USD currency pairs):

CHF/JPY	85.14/19
EUR/CHF	1.5676/78
EUR/GBP	0.6915/17
EUR/JPY	133.51/54
GBP/CHF	2.2666/74
GBP/JPY	193.02/10

The fact that the USD is the base currency in two of the pairs (USD/CHF and USD/JPY) and is the quote currency in two other pairs (EUR/USD and GBP/USD) plays an important role in the arithmetic of arbitrage. We begin our investigation with just the bid prices (see Table 15.2).

TABLE 15.2 Formulas for Cross Currencies		
CHFJPY = USDJPY / USDCHF	85.14 = 105.61 / 1.2402	85.1556
EURCHF = EURUSD × USDCHF	1.5676 = 1.2638 × 1.2402	1.567365
EURGBP = EURUSD / GBPUSD	0.6915 = 1.2638 / 1.8275	0.691546
EURJPY = EURUSD × USDJPY	133.51 = 1.2638 × 105.61	133.4699
GBPCHF = GBPUSD × USDCHF	2.2666 = 1.8275 × 1.2402	2.266466
GBPJPY = GBPUSD × USDJPY	193.02 = 1.8275 × 105.61	193.0023

TABLE 15.3	Calculations for Cross Currencies			
Pair	Rate	Calculation	Deviation	Pip Values
CHFJPY	85.1556	−85.14	= +0.0156	+1.56 pips
EURCHF	1.567365	−1.5676	= −0.000235	−2.35 pips
EURGBP	0.691546	−0.6915	= +0.000046	+0.46 pips
EURJPY	133.4699	−133.51	= −0.0401	−4.01 pips
GBPCHF	2.266466	−2.2666	= +0.000134	+1.34 pips
GBPJPY	193.0023	−193.02	= −0.0177	−1.77 pips

The criterion whether to multiply or divide the USD pairs in order to calculate the cross rate is simple:

- If the USD is the base currency in both pairs then divide the USD pairs.
- If the USD is the quote currency in both pairs then divide the USD pairs.
- Otherwise multiply the USD pairs.

To determine the deviation from parity for each cross pair, subtract the exchange rate from the calculated rate and convert the floating point decimals to pip values (see Table 15.3).

From the information in Table 15.3, we can see that the EUR/JPY is out of parity by four pips. To determine if an arbitrage opportunity is profitable, we must first calculate the total transaction cost by adding the three bid/ask spreads of the corresponding pairs:

$$\begin{array}{ll} \text{EUR/USD} & 2 \\ \text{USD/JPY} & +3 \\ \text{EUR/JPY} & \underline{+3} \\ & 8 \end{array}$$

An eight-pip transaction cost to earn a four-pip profit is counterproductive—it amounts to a four-pip loss. If the parity deviation (the number of pips by which the three currency pairs are out of alignment) were greater—say, 30 pips—then a definite arbitrage opportunity exists.

The trading mechanism to take advantage of this anomaly requires some consideration. First, determine what market actions are necessary to correct this anomaly. Assume that the EUR/JPY rate is currently trading at 133.51 and the calculated rate using the current EUR/USD and USD/JPY pairs is 133.81 (a 30-pip deviation). Parity between the three currencies will be restored if the following price action occurs:

(A) The EUR/JPY pair rises to 133.81, or

(B) The product of the EUR/USD and USD/JPY pairs drops to 133.51.

Therefore the following trades are required to "lock in" the 30-pip profit:

- Buy one lot of the EUR/JPY pair.
- Sell one lot of the EUR/USD pair.
- Sell one lot of the USD/JPY pair.
- Liquidate all three trades simultaneously when parity is reestablished.

Note: Executing only one or two "legs" of the three trades required in an arbitrage package does not guarantee a profit and may be quite dangerous. All three trades must be executed simultaneously before the "locked-in" profit can be realized.

Example 2

Two USD pairs and one cross pair (divide)   Example 1 used the product of the two USD currencies to calculate the cross rate. Now let's take an example of the ratio of the two USD currencies. Assume the EUR/GBP cross pair is currently trading at 0.6992 and that the ratio between the EUR/USD and GBP/USD pairs is calculated as 0.6952, a 40-pip deviation. Parity will be restored when the following price actions occur:

(A) The EUR/GBP pair drops to 0.6952, or

(B) The ratio of the EUR/USD and GBP/USD pairs rises to 0.6992.

In order for the second action to rise, either the EUR/USD pair must also rise or the GBP/USD pair must decline (this differs from the previous example). Therefore the following trades are required to realize a 40-pip profit:

- Sell one lot of the EUR/GBP pair.
- Buy one lot of the EUR/USD pair.
- Sell one lot of the GBP/USD pair.
- Liquidate all three trades the moment that parity is reestablished.

Example 3

Three non-USD cross pairs   Technically the arbitrage strategy can be performed on three non-USD currency pairs. In this example, we examine a straddle between the three European majors (EUR, GBP, CHF) while focusing on the EUR/CHF pair in respect to the two GBP currency pairs (GBP/CHF and EUR/GBP).

Assume the current rates of exchange are:

$$EUR/CHF = 1.5676/78$$
$$EUR/GBP = 0.6915/17$$
$$GBP/CHF = 2.2604/12$$

and their relationship is:

$$EUR/CHF = EUR/GBP \times GBP/CHF$$

Thus the calculated value for the EUR/CHF rate is 0.6915×2.2604 or 1.5631. The deviation from parity is $-.0045$ ($1.5631 - 1.5676$), or 45 CHF pips, since CHF is the pip currency in the EUR/CHF pair. The trading strategy is:

- Sell one lot of EUR/CHF.
- Buy one lot of EUR/GBP.
- Buy one lot of GBP/CHF.
- Liquidate all three when parity is reestablished.

If all three trades are executed successfully, a profit of 45 CHF pips is realized. Subtract the three bid/ask spreads for the transaction costs ($2 + 2 + 8 = 12$) to see a net profit of 33 CHF pips. Now convert CHF pips to dollars (33 divided by the USD/CHF rate, 1.2402) to obtain 27 USD pips.

Adding Complexity

It should be noted that in all the examples presented here that only three currencies are analyzed simultaneously. It is possible to add a fourth or even fifth currency to the mix, though this is normally left to the very serious arbitrage strategists.

The methodology for examining four (or even five) currencies at one time is to calculate every possible three-currency combination among the currencies selected. Rearrange them in order of magnitude of deviation from parity. Examine the deviations closely to see if there is a single anomaly or possibly even a double anomaly among the four currencies. This type of scrutiny will then determine if a four-currency arbitrage opportunity exists.

Specialized software is definitely required when dealing with four or more currencies in a single arbitrage package.

Pros and Cons of Arbitrage

Using triangular arbitrage strategies on the FOREX market has one very salient advantage: predetermined profits can be realized if the trades execute smoothly. Unfortunately, the disadvantages of this strategy are numerous:

- **Higher transaction costs.** The trader must pay the bid/ask spreads on three separate trades.
- **Higher margin requirements.** Roughly three times the margin is necessary to execute the arbitrage strategy and odd-lot trading may be required for the small-capital investor.
- **Precision timing is required.** Arbitrage opportunities are usually short-lived.
- **Complexity.** The trader must thoroughly understand the arbitrage mechanism in order to determine which currency pairs to buy and which to sell. Each arbitrage "package" consists of two buys and one sell or one buy and two sells. Miscalculating any one of the three trades can cause disaster.
- **Advanced monitoring techniques are usually required.** This means calculating the above analysis on several pairs simultaneously in real time. You will need a software program that analyzes streaming quotes continually. It is possible to perform these tasks manually but the trader must have a high tolerance for tedium.

We must also mention that in the examples in this chapter, we intentionally simplified calculations by using only the bid price throughout. When executing an actual arbitrage trade, the investor must supply both bid and ask rate where applicable.

Further Studies

If you are interested in delving deeper into the topics above for the purpose of including them in your personalized trading strategy, we recommend that (a) you contact your FOREX broker for detailed information and (b) review the texts and Web sites listed in Appendix F.

List of World Currencies and Symbols

Table A.1 is a list of global currencies and the three-character currency codes that we have found are generally used to represent them. Often, but not always, this code is the same as the ISO 4217 standard. (The ISO, or International Organization for Standardization, is a worldwide federation of national standards.)

In most cases, the currency code is composed of the country's two-character Internet country code plus an extra character to denote the currency unit. For example, the code for Canadian dollars is simply Canada's two-character Internet code ("CA") plus a one-character currency designator ("D").

We have endeavored to list the codes that, in our experience, are actually in general industry use to represent the currencies. Currency names are given in the plural form. This list does not contain obsolete Euro-zone currencies.

TABLE A.1	Symbol, Place, Currency Name	
AED	United Arab Emirates	Dirhams
AFA	Afghanistan	Afghanis
ALL	Albania	Leke
AMD	Armenia	Drams
ANG	Netherlands Antilles	Guilders
AOA	Angola	Kwanza

(continued on next page)

	TABLE A.1 *(continued)*	
ARS	Argentina	Pesos
AUD	Australia	Dollars
AWG	Aruba	Guilders
AZM	Azerbaijan	Manats
BAM	Bosnia, Herzegovina	Convertible Marka
BBD	Barbados	Dollars
BDT	Bangladesh	Taka
BGN	Bulgaria	Leva
BHD	Bahrain	Dinars
BIF	Burundi	Francs
BMD	Bermuda	Dollars
BND	Brunei Darussalam	Dollars
BOB	Bolivia	Bolivianos
BRL	Brazil	Brazil Real
BSD	Bahamas	Dollars
BTN	Bhutan	Ngultrum
BWP	Botswana	Pulas
BYR	Belarus	Rubles
BZD	Belize	Dollars
CAD	Canada	Dollars
CDF	Congo/Kinshasa	Congolese Francs
CHF	Switzerland	Francs
CLP	Chile	Pesos
CNY	China	Renminbi
COP	Colombia	Pesos
CRC	Costa Rica	Colones
CUP	Cuba	Pesos
CVE	Cape Verde	Escudos
CYP	Cyprus	Pounds
CZK	Czech Republic	Koruny
DJF	Djibouti	Francs
DKK	Denmark	Kroner
DOP	Dominican Republic	Pesos
DZD	Algeria	Algeria Dinars
EEK	Estonia	Krooni

	TABLE A.1 *(continued)*	
EGP	Egypt	Pounds
ERN	Eritrea	Nakfa
ETB	Ethiopia	Birr
EUR	Euro Member Countries	Euro
FJD	Fiji	Dollars
FKP	Falkland Islands	Pounds
GBP	United Kingdom	Pounds
GEL	Georgia	Lari
GGP	Guernsey	Pounds
GHC	Ghana	Cedis
GIP	Gibraltar	Pounds
GMD	Gambia	Dalasi
GNF	Guinea	Francs
GTQ	Guatemala	Quetzales
GYD	Guyana	Dollars
HKD	Hong Kong	Dollars
HNL	Honduras	Lempiras
HRK	Croatia	Kuna
HTG	Haiti	Gourdes
HUF	Hungary	Forint
IDR	Indonesia	Rupiahs
ILS	Israel	New Shekels
IMP	Isle of Man	Pounds
INR	India	Rupees
IQD	Iraq	Dinars
IRR	Iran	Rials
ISK	Iceland	Kronur
JEP	Jersey	Pounds
JMD	Jamaica	Dollars
JOD	Jordan	Dinars
JPY	Japan	Yen
KES	Kenya	Shillings
KGS	Kyrgyzstan	Soms
KHR	Cambodia	Riels
KMF	Comoros	Francs

(continued on next page)

TABLE A.1 *(continued)*

KPW	Korea (North)	Won
KRW	Korea (South)	Won
KWD	Kuwait	Dinars
KYD	Cayman Islands	Dollars
KZT	Kazakstan	Tenge
LAK	Laos	Kips
LBP	Lebanon	Pounds
LKR	Sri Lanka	Rupees
LRD	Liberia	Dollars
LSL	Lesotho	Maloti
LTL	Lithuania	Litai
LVL	Latvia	Lati
LYD	Libya	Dinars
MAD	Morocco	Dirhams
MDL	Moldova	Lei
MGA	Madagascar	Ariary
MKD	Macedonia	Denars
MMK	Myanmar (Burma)	Kyats
MNT	Mongolia	Tugriks
MOP	Macau	Patacas
MRO	Mauritania	Ouguiyas
MTL	Malta	Liri
MUR	Mauritius	Rupees
MVR	Maldives	Rufiyaa
MWK	Malawi	Kwachas
MXN	Mexico	Pesos
MYR	Malaysia	Ringgits
MZM	Mozambique	Meticais
NAD	Namibia	Dollars
NGN	Nigeria	Nairas
NIO	Nicaragua	Gold Cordobas
NOK	Norway	Krone
NPR	Nepal	Nepal Rupees
NZD	New Zealand	Dollars
OMR	Oman	Rials

	TABLE A.1 *(continued)*	
PAB	Panama	Balboa
PEN	Peru	Nuevos Soles
PGK	Papua New Guinea	Kina
PHP	Philippines	Pesos
PKR	Pakistan	Rupees
PLN	Poland	Zlotych
PYG	Paraguay	Guarani
QAR	Qatar	Rials
ROL	Romania	Lei
RUR	Russia	Rubles
RWF	Rwanda	Rwanda Francs
SAR	Saudi Arabia	Riyals
SBD	Solomon Islands	Dollars
SCR	Seychelles	Rupees
SDD	Sudan	Dinars
SEK	Sweden	Kronor
SGD	Singapore	Dollars
SHP	Saint Helena	Pounds
SIT	Slovenia	Tolars
SKK	Slovakia	Koruny
SLL	Sierra Leone	Leones
SOS	Somalia	Shillings
SPL	Seborga	Luigini
SRG	Suriname	Guilders
STD	São Tome, Principe	Dobras
SVC	El Salvador	Colones
SYP	Syria	Pounds
SZL	Swaziland	Emalangeni
THB	Thailand	Baht
TJS	Tajikistan	Somoni
TMM	Turkmenistan	Manats
TND	Tunisia	Dinars
TOP	Tonga	Pa'anga
TRL	Turkey	Liras
TTD	Trinidad, Tobago	Dollars

(continued on next page)

TABLE A.1   *(continued)*

TVD	Tuvalu	Tuvalu Dollars
TWD	Taiwan	New Dollars
TZS	Tanzania	Shillings
UAH	Ukraine	Hryvnia
UGX	Uganda	Shillings
USD	United States of America	Dollars
UYU	Uruguay	Pesos
UZS	Uzbekistan	Sums
VEB	Venezuela	Bolivares
VND	Viet Nam	Dong
VUV	Vanuatu	Vatu
WST	Samoa	Tala
XAF	Communauté Financière Africaine	Francs
XAG	Silver	Ounces
XAU	Gold	Ounces
XCD	East Caribbean	Dollars
XDR	International Monetary Fund	Special Drawing Rights
XOF	Communauté Financière Africaine	Francs
XPD	Palladium	Ounces
XPF	Comptoirs Français du Pacifique	Francs
XPT	Platinum	Ounces
YER	Yemen	Rials
YUM	Yugoslavia	New Dinars
ZAR	South Africa	Rand
ZMK	Zambia	Kwacha
ZWD	Zimbabwe	Zimbabwe Dollars

Exchange Rates

Table B.1 shows the foreign exchange rates on 7/1/2004 compared with the USD.

TABLE B.1	Exchange Rates		
	ISO Currency	*USD/Unit*	*Units/USD*
TRL	Turkish Lira	0.0000	1428571
ROL	Romanian Leu	0.0000	33333.3
IDR	Indonesian Rupiah	0.0001	8695.65
ZMK	Zambian Kwacha	0.0002	4739.33
VEB	Venezuelan Bolivar	0.0005	1923.07
LBP	Lebanese Pounds	0.0007	1512.85
KRW	South Korean Won	0.0009	1155.34
CLP	Chilean Pesos	0.0016	623.441
SDD	Sudan Dinar	0.0038	263.157
HUF	Hungarian Forint	0.0048	210.084
JPY	Japanese Yen	0.0092	108.607
ISK	Icelandic Krona	0.0136	73.7463

(continued on next page)

TABLE B.1 *(continued)*

ISO Currency		USD/Unit	Units/USD
DZD	Algerian Dinars	0.0141	70.9220
JMD	Jamaican Dollars	0.0167	60.0601
PKR	Pakistani Rupees	0.0175	57.2738
PHP	Filipino Pesos	0.0180	55.6793
INR	Indian Rupees	0.0223	44.7828
THB	Thai Bhat	0.0250	40.0000
SKK	Slovakian Koruna	0.0296	33.7838
TWD	Taiwanese Dollars	0.0298	33.6022
RUR	Russian Rubles	0.0345	29.0189
CZK	Czech Koruna	0.0367	27.2480
MXP	Mexican Pesos	0.0871	11.4806
CNY	Chinese Renminbi	0.1208	8.2781
HKD	Hong Kong Dollars	0.1282	7.8004
SEK	Swedish Krona	0.1340	7.4623
NOK	Norway Kroner	0.1445	6.9208
EGP	Egyptian Pounds	0.1618	6.1805
TTD	Trinidad/Tobago Dollars	0.1626	6.1501
ZAR	South African Rand	0.1637	6.1104
DKK	Danish Kroner	0.1650	6.0611
ILS	Israeli New Shekels	0.2236	4.4728
PLZ	Polish Zloty	0.2510	3.9811
MYR	Malaysian Ringgit	0.2632	3.7994
SAR	Saudi Arabian Riyal	0.2666	3.7503
BRL	Brazilian Real	0.3381	2.9577
ARP	Argentinean Pesos	0.3515	2.8450
BBD	Barbados Dollars	0.5025	1.9900
FJD	Fiji Dollars	0.5670	1.7637
SGD	Singapore Dollars	0.5834	1.7141
BGL	Bulgarian Lev	0.6133	1.6305
NZD	New Zealand Dollars	0.6464	1.5470
AUD	Australian Dollars	0.7128	1.4029
CAD	Canadian Dollars	0.7543	1.3257
CHF	Swiss Francs	0.8097	1.2351

TABLE B.1		(continued)	
	ISO Currency	*USD/Unit*	*Units/USD*
SD	Bahamas Dollars	1.0000	1.0000
BMD	Bermudan Dollars	1.0000	1.0000
USD	United States Dollars	1.0000	1.0000
EUR	Eurocurrency	1.2309	0.8124
JOD	Jordanian Dinar	1.4129	0.7080
GBP	United Kingdom Pounds	1.8031	0.5464
CYP	Cyprus Pounds	2.0375	0.4908

Rates quoted from the Bank of Montréal and ExchangeRate.com.

Euro Currency Unit

On January 1, 1999, eleven of the countries in the European Economic and Monetary Union (EMU) decided to give up their own currencies and adopt the new Euro (EUR) currency: Austria, Belgium, Finland, France, Germany, Ireland, Italy, Luxembourg, the Netherlands, Portugal, and Spain. Greece followed suit on January 1, 2001. The Vatican City also participated in the changeover. This changeover is now complete.

It is worth noting that any place that previously used one or more of the currencies listed below has now also adopted the Euro. This applies to the Principality of Andorra, the Principality of Monaco, and the Republic of San Marino. This of course applies automatically to any territories, departments, possessions, or collectivities of Euro-zone countries, such as the Azores, Balearic Islands, the Canary Islands, Europa Island, French Guiana, Guadeloupe, Juan de Nova, the Madeira Islands, Martinique, Mayotte, Réunion, Saint-Martin, Saint Pierre, and Miquelon, to name just a few.

Euro bank notes and coins began circulating in the above countries on January 1, 2002. At that time, all transactions in those countries were valued in Euro, and the "old" notes and coins of these countries were gradually withdrawn from circulation. The precise dates that each "old" currency ceased being legal tender are noted in Table C.1.

For convenience, and because their values are now irrevocably set against the Euro as listed in Table C.1, the XE.com Universal Currency Converter will continue to support these units even after their withdrawal from circulation. In

TABLE C.1   Official Fixed Euro Rates for Participating Countries

Legacy (Old) Currency			Conversion to Euro	Conversion from Euro
ATS	Austria	Schilling	ATS / 13.7603 = EUR	EUR × 13.7603 = ATS
BEF	Belgium	Franc	BEF / 40.3399 = EUR	EUR × 40.3399 = BEF
DEM	Germany	Mark	DEM / 1.95583 = EUR	EUR × 1.95583 = DEM
ESP	Spain	Peseta	ESP / 166.386 = EUR	EUR × 166.386 = ESP
FIM	Finland	Markka	FIM / 5.94573 = EUR	EUR × 5.94573 = FIM
FRF	France	Franc	FRF / 6.55957 = EUR	EUR × 6.55957 = FRF
GRD	Greece	Drachma	GRD / 340.750 = EUR	EUR × 340.750 = GRD
IEP	Ireland	Punt	IEP / 0.787564 = EUR	EUR × 0.787564 = IEP
ITL	Italy	Lira	ITL / 1936.27 = EUR	EUR × 1936.27 = ITL
LUF	Luxembourg	Franc	LUF / 40.3399 = EUR	EUR × 40.3399 = LUF
NLG	Netherlands	Guilder	NLG / 2.20371 = EUR	EUR × 2.20371 = NLG
PTE	Portugal	Escudo	PTE / 200.482 = EUR	EUR × 200.482 = PTE
VAL	Vatican City	Lira	VAL / 1936.27 = EUR	EUR × 1936.27 = VAL

addition, most outgoing Euro currencies will still be physically convertible at special locations for a period of several years. For details, refer to the official Euro site, www.europa.eu.int/euro.

Also note that the Euro is not just the same thing as the former European Currency Unit (or "ECU"), which used to be listed as "XEU". The ECU was a theoretical "basket" of currencies rather than a currency itself, and no "ECU" bank notes or coins ever existed. At any rate, the ECU has been replaced by the Euro, which is a bona fide currency.

A note about spelling and capitalization: the official spelling of the EUR currency unit in the English language is "euro", with a lower case "e." However, the overwhelmingly prevailing industry practice is to spell it "Euro," with a capital "E." Since other currency names are capitalized in general use, doing so helps differentiate the noun "Euro," meaning EUR currency, from the more general adjective "euro," meaning anything even remotely having to do with Europe.

Appendix D

Time Zones and Global Banking Hours

The following table emphasizes the importance of the effect of time of day on FOREX market activity and volatility based on hours of operation around the globe. The top row is Greenwich Mean Time expressed in 24-hour military format. Banking hours are arbitrarily assumed to be 9:00 AM to 4:00 PM around the globe. See Figure D.1

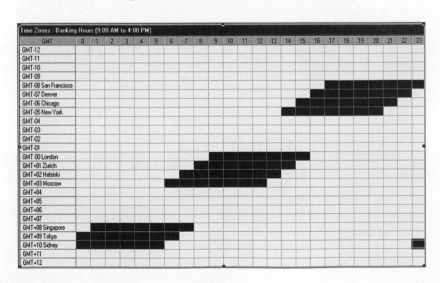

FIGURE D.1   Global banking hours.

Examples of chart usage are:

- Locate Denver (row 6, or GMT less 7 hours). The first darkened cell in this row indicates when Denver banks open relative to other world banks.

- Move upward to top row to see that the concurrent time in London is 17:00 or 5:00 PM, where British banks are now closed.

- A FOREX trader in New York must trade between 3:00 AM to 11:00 AM Eastern Standard Time in order to follow the heightened activity in central European markets (GMT+1: Zurich, Frankfurt, Vienna, Copenhagen).

- San Francisco banks are closing while Sidney banks are opening, and so on.

The darkened areas in Figure D.1 accentuate the major banking centers. FOREX is a 24-hour market. You can trade 24 hours a day.

Appendix E

Central Banks and Regulatory Agencies

A brief history of currency regulation is provided in Chapter 2 of this book. Traders interested in more details may visit the Web sites listed in Table E.1.

The complete text of the "Commodity Futures Modernization Act 2000" in Adobe PDF format can be accessed at the following Web site: *www. cftc.gov/ files/ogc/ogchr5660.pdf.*

Table E.2 is a list of affiliated central banks by country.

TABLE E.1	Regulatory Agencies
Federal Reserve System	*www.federalreserve.gov*
Federal Reserve Bank	*www.ny.frb.org*
Securities and Exchange Commission	*www.sec.gov*
Commodity Futures Trading Commission	*www.cftc.gov*
National Futures Association	*www.nfa.futures.org*
Financial Services Authority	*www.fsa.gov.uk*
Australian Securities & Investments Commission	*www.asic.gov.au/asic/asic.nsf*
Bank of International Settlements	*www.bis.org*
Regulation in Canada	*www.ida.ca/Investors/SecRegulation_en.asp*

TABLE E.2 Central Banks

Argentina	Banco Central de la Republica Argentina
Armenia	Central Bank of Armenia
Aruba	Centrale Bank van Aruba
Australia	Reserve Bank of Australia
Austria	Oesterreichische Nationalbank
Bahrain	Bahrain Monetary Agency
Belgium	Banque Nationale de Belgique
Benin	Banque Centrale des Etats de l'Afrique de l'Ouest
Bolivia	Banco Central de Bolivia
Bosnia	Central Bank of Bosnia and Herzegovina
Botswana	Bank of Botswana
Brazil	Banco Central do Brasil
Bulgaria	Bulgarian National Bank
Burkina Faso	Banque Centrale des Etats de l'Afrique de l'Ouest
Canada	Bank of Canada
Chile	Banco Central de Chil
China	Peoples Bank of China
Colombia	Banco de la Republic
Costa Rica	Banco Central de Costa Rica
Côte d'Ivoire	Banque Centrale des Etats de l'Afrique de l'Ouest
Croatia	Croatian National Bank
Cyprus	Central Bank of Cyprus
Czech Republic	Ceska Narodni Banka
Denmark	Danmarks Nationalbank
East Caribbean	The East Caribbean Central Bank
Ecuador	Banco Central del Ecuador
Egypt	Central Bank of Egypt
El Salvador	The Central Reserve Bank of El Salvador
Estonia	Eesti Pank
European Union	European Central Bank
Finland	Suomen Pankki
France	Banque de France
Germany	Deutsche Bundesbank
Greece	Bank of Greece

TABLE E.2 *(continued)*	
Guatemala	Banco de Guatemala
Guinea Bissau	Banque Centrale des Etats de l'Afrique de l'Ouest
Hong Kong	Hong Kong Monetary Authority
Hungary	National Bank of Hungary
Iceland	Central Bank of Iceland
India	Reserve Bank of India
Indonesia	Bank of Indonesia
Ireland	Central Bank of Ireland
Israel	Bank of Israel
Italy	Banca d'Italia
Jamaica	Bank of Jamaica
Japan	Bank of Japan
Jordan	Central Bank of Jordan
Kenya	Central Bank of Kenya
Korea	Bank of Korea
Kuwait	Central Bank of Kuwait
Latvia	Bank of Latvia
Lebanon	Banque du Liban
Lithuania	Lietuvos Bankas
Luxembourg	Banque Centrale du Luxemburg
Macedonia	National Bank of the Republic of Macedonia
Malaysia	Bank Negara Malaysia
Mali	Banque Centrale des Etats de l'Afrique de l'Ouest
Malta	Central Bank of Malta
Mauritius	Bank of Mauritius
Mexico	Banco de Mexico
Moldova	The National Bank of Moldova
Mozambique	Bank of Mozambique
Namibia	Bank of Namibia
Netherlands	De Nederlandsche Bank
Netherlands Antilles	Bank van de Nederlandse Antillen
New Zealand	Reserve Bank of New Zealand
Niger	Banque Centrale des Etats de l'Afrique de l'Ouest
Norway	Norges Bank

(continued on next page)

TABLE E.2 *(continued)*

Paraguay	Banco Central del Paraguay
Peru	Banco Central de Reserva del Peru
Poland	National Bank of Poland
Portugal	Banco de Portugal
Qatar	Qatar Central Bank
Romania	National Bank of Romania
Russia	Central Bank of Russia
Saudi Arabia	Saudi Arabian Monetary Agency
Senegal	Banque Centrale des Etats de l'Afrique de l'Ouest
Singapore	Monetary Authority of Singapore
Slovakia	National Bank of Slovakia
Slovenia	Bank of Slovenia
South Africa	The South African Reserve Bank
Spain	Banco de España
Sri Lanka	Central Bank of Sri Lanka
Sweden	Sveriges Riksbank
Switzerland	Schweizerische Nationalbank
Tanzania	Bank of Tanzania
Thailand	Bank of Thailand
Togo	Banque Centrale des Etats de l'Afrique de l'Ouest
Trinidad and Tobago	Central Bank of Trinidad and Tobago
Tunisia	Banque Centrale de Tunisie
Turkey	Türkiye Cumhuriyet Merkez Bankasi
Ukraine	National Bank of Ukraine
United Kingdom	Bank of England
United States	Board of Governors of the Federal Reserve System
Zambia	Bank of Zambia
Zimbabwe	Reserve Bank of Zimbabwe

Central bank Web sites may be found at *www.bis.org/cbanks.htm.*

Resources

Periodicals

Though the following monthly magazines focus on very specific material, each frequently prints very informative and timely articles on the FOREX marketplace:

Active Trader (TechInfo, Inc.)—*www.activetradermag.com*

Futures (Futures Magazine, Inc.)—*www.futuresmag.com*

Technical Analysis of Stocks & Commodities (Technical Analysis, Inc.)—*www.traders.com*

Books

The following list, though in no way complete, provides traders with FOREX library essentials:

Henderson, Callum, *Currency Strategy* (Wiley) 2002.

Klopfenstein, Gary, *Trading Currency Cross Rates* (Wiley) 1993.

Louw, G. N., *Begin Forex* (FXTrader) 2003.

Luca, Cornelius, *Technical Analysis Applications in the Global Currency Markets* (Prentice Hall) 2000.

Luca, Cornelius, *Trading in the Global Currency Markets* (Prentice Hall) 2000.

Murphy, John, *Intermarket Financial Analysis* (Wiley) 1999.

Murphy, John, *Technical Analysis of the Financial Markets* (Prentice Hall) 1999.

Reuters Limited, *An Introduction to Foreign Exchange and Money Markets* (Reuters Financial Training) 1999.

Shamah, Shani, *A Foreign Exchange Primer* (Wiley) 2003.

There are hundreds (if not thousands) of books pertaining specifically to technical analysis. A few of the most well-known are:

Aby, Carroll D, Jr., PhD, *Point and Figure Charting* (Traders Press) 1996.

Bickford, Jim, *Chart Plotting Algorithms for Technical Analysts* (Syzygy) 2002.

McGee, John, *Technical Analysis of Stock Trends* (American Management Association) 2001.

Nison, Steve, *Japanese Candlestick Charting Techniques* (Hall) 2001.

A fine resource for finding more titles is *http://www.traderspress.com*.

Web Sites

We encourage the trader to visit the following Web sites for additional information on trading currencies. These sites are provided for research purposes. The amount of information on currency trading now on the Internet is enormous: A Google search finds over 2.2 million entries for "forex." Inclusion herein *does not* represent an endorsement of any kind.

Online Brokers and Dealers

www.cbfx.com

www.ac-markets.com

www.refcofx.com

www.saxobank.com

www.gftforex.com

www.hotspotfx.com

www.cmc-forex.com

www.cms-forex.com

www.oanda.com

www.sbfx.com

www.fxall.com

Data

ozforex.tradesecuring.com/misc/ozchart.asp

www.csidata.com

www.forexcapital.com/database.htm

www.olsendata.com

disktrading.is99.com/disktrading

www.cqg.com/products/datafactory.cfm

www.datastream.com/

www.tenfore.com/index.php?T4_Session=9b7d26531b2829babdb317083f8fe994

www.dukascopy.com

www.netdania.com

www.pctrader.com

Charts

www.esignal.com

www.dynexcorp.com/charts/eu1h.shtml

www.forex-markets.com/javacharts.htm

www.fxstreet.com/nou/graph/senseframeschartsnetdania.asp

www.forexcharts.com/

www.fxtrek.com

www.moneytec.com

www.global-view.com/beta/

www.fxstreet.com

www.forexdirectory.net

www.forex-markets.com

www.hantec.com.hk

www.business.com/directory/financial_services/investment_banking_and_ brokerage/ sales_and_trading/foreign_exchange

Portals and Forums

www.moneytec.com

www.investorsresource.info

www.global-view.com/beta

www.fxstreet.com

www.forexdirectory.net

www.forexvision.com

Software Development

www.snapdragon.co.uk

www.commtools.com

Link Pages

www.dynexcorp.com/links.shtml

www.forexdirectory.net

www.forex-brokers-list.com

www.investorsresource.info/portal.htm

Michael Archer's Web site offers an extensive, categorized "FOREX on the Internet" report:

www.commtools.com/p-online.html

Glossary

appreciation   a currency is said to appreciate when it strengthens in price in response to market demand.

arbitrage   the purchase or sale of an instrument and simultaneous taking of an equal and opposite position in a related market, in order to take advantage of small price differentials between markets.

ask price   the price at which the market is prepared to sell a specific currency in a foreign exchange contract or cross currency contract. At this price, the trader can buy the base currency. In the quotation, it is shown on the right side of the quotation. For example, in the quote USD/CHF 1.4527/32, the ask price is 1.4532; meaning you can buy one U.S. dollar for 1.4532 Swiss francs.

at best   an instruction given to a dealer to buy or sell at the best rate that can be obtained.

at or better   an order to deal at a specific rate or better.

balance of trade   the value of a country's exports minus its imports.

bar chart   a type of chart that consists of four significant points: the high and the low prices, which form the vertical bar, the opening price, which is marked with a small horizontal line to the left of the bar, and the closing price, which is marked with a small horizontal line to the right of the bar.

base currency   the first currency in a currency pair. It shows how much the base currency is worth as measured against the second currency. For example, if the USD/CHF rate equals 1.6215, then one USD is worth CHF 1.6215. In the FX markets, the U.S. dollar is normally considered the base currency for quotes, meaning that quotes are expressed as a unit of $1 USD per the other currency quoted in the pair. The primary exceptions to this rule are the British pound, the Euro, and the Australian dollar.

bear market   a market distinguished by declining prices.

bid price   the bid is the price at which the market is prepared to buy a specific currency in a foreign exchange contract or cross currency contract. At this price, the trader can sell the base currency. It is shown on the left side of the quotation. For example, in the quote USD/CHF 1.4527/32, the bid price is 1.4527, meaning you can sell one U.S. dollar for 1.4527 Swiss francs.

bid/ask spread   the difference between the bid and offer price.

big figure quote   dealer expression referring to the first few digits of an exchange rate. These digits are often omitted in dealer quotes. For example, a USD/JPY rate might be 117.30/117.35, but it would be quoted verbally without the first three digits, that is "30/35."

book   in a professional trading environment, a "book" is the summary of a trader's or desk's total positions.

broker   an individual or firm that acts as an intermediary, putting together buyers and sellers for a fee or commission. In contrast, a *dealer* commits capital and takes one side of a position, hoping to earn a spread (profit) by closing out the position in a subsequent trade with another party.

Bretton Woods agreement of 1944   an agreement that established fixed foreign exchange rates for major currencies, provided for central bank intervention in the currency markets, and pegged the price of gold at US $35 per ounce. The agreement lasted until 1971, when President Nixon overturned the Bretton Woods agreement and established a floating exchange rate for the major currencies.

bull market   a market distinguished by rising prices.

bundesbank   germany's Central Bank.

cable   trader jargon referring to the sterling/U.S. dollar exchange rate, so called because the rate was originally transmitted via a transatlantic cable beginning in the mid 1800s.

candlestick chart   a chart that indicates the trading range for the day as well as the opening and closing price. If the open price is higher than the close price, the rectangle between the open and close price is shaded. If the close price is higher than the open price, that area of the chart is not shaded.

cash market   the market in the actual financial instrument on which a futures or options contract is based.

central bank   a government or quasi-governmental organization that manages a country's monetary policy. For example, the U.S. central bank is the Federal Reserve, and the German central bank is the Bundesbank.

chartist   an individual who uses charts and graphs and interprets historical data to find trends and predict future movements. Also referred to as technical trader.

cleared funds   funds that are freely available, sent in to settle a trade.

closed position   exposures in foreign currencies that no longer exist. The process to close a position is to sell or buy a certain amount of currency to offset an equal amount of the open position. This will "square" the position.

clearing   the process of settling a trade.

collateral   something given to secure a loan or as a guarantee of performance.

commission   a transaction fee charged by a broker.

confirmation   a document exchanged by counterparts to a transaction that states the terms of said transaction.

contagion   the tendency of an economic crisis to spread from one market to another. In 1997, political instability in Indonesia caused high volatility in its domestic currency, the Rupiah. From there, the contagion spread to other Asian emerging currencies, and then to Latin America, and is now referred to as the "Asian Contagion."

contract   the standard unit of trading.

counter currency   the second listed currency in a currency pair.

counterparty   one of the participants in a financial transaction.

country risk   risk associated with a cross-border transaction, including, but not limited to, legal and political conditions.

cross currency pair   a foreign exchange transaction in which one foreign currency is traded against a second foreign currency—for example, EUR/GBP.

cross rate   same as cross currency pair.

currency   any form of money issued by a government or central bank and used as legal tender and a basis for trade.

currency pair   the two currencies that make up a foreign exchange rate—for example, EUR/USD.

currency risk   the probability of an adverse change in exchange rates.

day trader   speculators who take positions in currencies that are then liquidated prior to the close of the same trading day.

dealer   an individual or firm that acts as a principal or counterpart to a transaction. Principals take one side of a position, hoping to earn a spread (profit) by closing out the position in a subsequent trade with another party. In contrast, a broker is an individual or firm that acts as an intermediary, putting together buyers and sellers for a fee or commission.

deficit   a negative balance of trade or payments.

delivery   an FX trade where both sides make and take actual delivery of the currencies traded.

depreciation   a fall in the value of a currency due to market forces.

derivative   a contract that changes in value in relation to the price movements of a related or underlying security, future, or other physical instrument. An option is the most common derivative instrument.

devaluation   the deliberate downward adjustment of a currency's price, normally by official announcement.

economic indicator   a government-issued statistic that indicates current economic growth and stability. Some common indicators are employment rates, gross domestic product (GDP), inflation, and retail sales.

end of day order (EOD)   an order to buy or sell at a specified price. This order remains open until the end of the trading day, which is typically 5 PM EST.

European Monetary Union (EMU)   the principal goal of the EMU is to establish a single European currency called the Euro, which will officially replace the national currencies of the EU member countries in 2002. On Janaury 1, 1999, the transitional phase to introduce the Euro began. The Euro now exists as a banking currency and paper financial transactions and foreign exchange are made in Euros. This transition period will last for three years, at which time Euro notes and coins will enter circulation. On July 1, 2002, only Euros will be legal tender for EMU participants, the national currencies of the member countries will cease to exist. The current members of the EMU are Germany, France, Belgium, Luxembourg, Austria, Finland, Ireland, the Netherlands, Italy, Spain, and Portugal.

Euro   the currency of the European Monetary Union (EMU). A replacement for the European Currency Unit (ECU).

European Central Bank (ECB)   the central bank for the new European Monetary Union.

Federal Deposit Insurance Corporation (FDIC)   the regulatory agency responsible for administering bank depository insurance in the United States.

Federal Reserve (Fed)   the central bank for the United States.

First In First Out (FIFO)   open positions are closed according to the FIFO accounting rule. All positions opened within a particular currency pair are liquidated in the order in which they were originally opened.

flat/square   dealer jargon used to describe a position that has been completely reversed—for example, you bought $500,000 then sold $500,000, thereby creating a neutral (flat) position.

foreign exchange (FOREX, FX)   the simultaneous buying of one currency and selling of another.

forward   the prespecified exchange rate for a foreign exchange contract settling at some agreed future date, based upon the interest rate differential between the two currencies involved.

forward points   the pips added to or subtracted from the current exchange rate to calculate a forward price.

fundamental analysis   analysis of economic and political information with the objective of determining future movements in a financial market.

futures contract   an obligation to exchange a good or instrument at a set price at a future date. The primary difference between a future and a forward is that futures are typically traded over an exchange (exchange-traded contacts, ETC), whereas forwards are considered over the counter (OTC) contracts. An OTC is any contract *not* traded on an exchange.

FX   Foreign exchange.

G8   the eight leading industrial countries that meet annually to evaluate and coordinate economic policy: the United States, Germany, Japan, France, the United Kingdom, Canada, Italy, and Russia.

going long   the purchase of a stock, commodity, or currency for investment or speculation.

going short   the selling of a currency or instrument not owned by the seller.

gross domestic product (GDP)   total value of a country's output, income, or expenditure produced within the country's physical borders.

gross national product (GNP)   gross domestic product plus income earned from investment or work abroad.

good 'til canceled order (GTC)   an order to buy or sell at a specified price. This order remains open until filled or until the client cancels.

hedge   a position or combination of positions that reduces the risk of your primary position.

"hit the bid"   acceptance of purchasing at the offer (ask) price or selling at the bid price.

inflation   an economic condition whereby prices for consumer goods rise, eroding purchasing power.

initial margin   the initial deposit of collateral required to enter into a position as a guarantee on future performance.

interbank rates   the foreign exchange rates at which large international banks quote other large international banks.

intervention   action by a central bank to affect the value of its currency by entering the market. Concerted intervention refers to action by a number of central banks to control exchange rates.

kiwi   slang for the New Zealand dollar.

leading indicators   statistics that are considered to predict future economic activity.

leverage   also called margin. The ratio of the amount used in a transaction to the required security deposit.

LIBOR   the London Inter-Bank Offered Rate. Banks use LIBOR when borrowing from another bank.

limit order   an order with restrictions on the maximum price to be paid or the minimum price to be received.

liquidation   the closing of an existing position through the execution of an offsetting transaction.

liquidity   the ability of a market to accept large transactions with minimal to no impact on price stability; also the ability to enter and exit a market quickly.

long position   a position that appreciates in value if market prices increase. When the base currency in the pair is bought, the position is said to be long.

lot   a unit to measure the amount of the deal. The value of the deal always corresponds to an integer number of lots.

margin   the required equity that an investor must deposit to collateralize a position.

margin call   a request from a broker or dealer for additional funds or other collateral to guarantee performance on a position that has moved against the customer.

market maker   a dealer who regularly quotes both bid and ask prices and is ready to make a two-sided market for any financial instrument.

market risk   exposure to changes in market prices.

mark-to-market   process of reevaluating all open positions with the current market prices. These new values then determine margin requirements.

maturity   the date for settlement or expiry of a financial instrument.

net position   the amount of currency bought or sold that has not yet been offset by opposite transactions.

offer   the rate at which a dealer is willing to sell a currency. See *ask price*.

offsetting transaction   a trade that serves to cancel or offset some or all of the market risk of an open position.

one cancels the other order (OCO)   a designation for two orders whereby when one part of the two orders is executed the other is automatically canceled.

open order   an order that will be executed when a market moves to its designated price. Normally associated with good 'til canceled orders.

open position   an active trade with corresponding unrealized profits and losses, which have not been offset by an equal and opposite deal.

order   an instruction to execute a trade at a specified rate.

over-the-counter (OTC)   used to describe any transaction that is not conducted over an exchange.

overnight position   a trade that remains open until the next business day.

pip   the smallest unit of price for any foreign currency. Digits added to or subtracted from the fourth decimal place, that is, 0.0001. Pips are also called points.

political risk   exposure to changes in governmental policy that will have an adverse effect on an investor's position.

position   the netted total holdings of a given currency.

premium   in the currency markets, describes the amount by which the forward or futures price exceed the spot price.

price transparency   describes quotes to which every market participant has equal access.

profit/loss or P/L or gain/loss   the actual realized gain or loss resulting from trading activities on closed positions, plus the theoretical "unrealized" gain or loss on open positions that have been mark-to-market.

quote   an indicative market price, normally used for information purposes only.

quote currency   the second currency in the currency pair. Price chenges in the currency pair are expressed in terms of the quote currency.

rally   a recovery in price after a period of decline.

range   the difference between the highest and lowest price of a future recorded during a given trading session.

rate   the price of one currency in terms of another, typically used for dealing purposes.

resistance   a term used in technical analysis indicating a specific price level at which analysis concludes people will sell.

revaluation   an increase in the exchange rate for a currency as a result of central bank intervention. Opposite of devaluation.

risk   exposure to uncertain change, most often used with a negative connotation of adverse change.

risk management   the employment of financial analysis and trading techniques to reduce and control exposure to various types of risk.

rollover   process whereby the settlement of a deal is rolled forward to another value date. The cost of this process is based on the interest rate differential of the two currencies.

round trip   the buying and selling of a specified amount of currency.

settlement   the process by which a trade is entered into the books and records of the counterparts to a transaction. The settlement of currency trades may or may not involve the actual physical exchange of one currency for another.

short position   an investment position that benefits from a decline in market price. When the base currency in the pair is sold, the position is said to be short.

spot price   the current market price. Settlement of spot transactions usually occurs within two business days.

spread   the difference between the bid and offer prices.

square   purchase and sales are in balance and thus the dealer has no open position.

sterling   slang for British Pound.

stop-loss order   order type whereby an open position is automatically liquidated at a specific price. Often used to minimize exposure to losses if the market moves against an investor's position. As an example, if an investor is long USD at 156.27, he or she might wish to put in a stop-loss order for 155.49, which would limit losses should the dollar depreciate, possibly below 155.49.

support levels   a technique used in technical analysis that indicates a specific price ceiling and floor at which a given exchange rate will automatically correct itself. Opposite of resistance.

swap   a currency swap is the simultaneous sale and purchase of the same amount of a given currency at a forward exchange rate.

swissy   market slang for Swiss franc.

technical analysis   an effort to forecast prices by analyzing market data, that is, historical price trends and averages, volumes, open interest, and so forth.

tick   a minimum change in time required for the price to change, up or down.

transaction cost   the cost of buying or selling a financial instrument.

transaction date   the date on which a trade occurs.

turnover   the total money value of all executed transactions in a given time period; volume.

two-way price   when both a bid and offer rate is quoted for an FX transaction.

unrealized gain/loss   the theoretical gain or loss on open positions valued at current market rates, as determined by the broker at its sole discretion. Unrealized gains/losses become profits/losses when position is closed.

uptick   a new price quote at a price higher than the preceding quote.

uptick rule   in the United States, a regulation whereby a security may not be sold short unless the last trade prior to the short sale was at a price lower than the price at which the short sale is executed.

U.S. prime rate   the interest rate at which United States banks will lend to their prime corporate customers.

value date   the date on which counterparts to a financial transaction agree to settle their respective obligations, that is, exchanging payments. For spot currency transactions, the value date is normally two business days forward. Also known as maturity date.

variation margin   funds that a broker must request from the client to have the required margin deposited. The term usually refers to additional funds that must be deposited as a result of unfavorable price movements.

volatility   a statistical measure of a market's price movements over time characterized by deviations from a predetermined central value (usually the arithmetic mean).

whipsaw   slang for the condition of when any securities market begins moving laterally and exhibits very little volatility.

yard   slang for a billion.

Index

About the Authors

Michael Duane Archer has been an active commodity futures and FOREX trader for over 30 years. Mike has also worked in various registered advisory capacities, notably as a CTA (Commodity Trading Advisor) and as an Investment Advisor. He is currently CEO of CommTools, Inc., a corporation focusing on nonlinear solutions to trend forecasting, with a special emphasis on cellular automata models.

James L. Bickford is a 27-year software engineering veteran, technical analyst, and a very active FOREX day trader with an academic background in applied mathematics and statistics. He has numerous books to his credit and recently published *Chart Plotting Algorithms for Technical Analysts*.

Edge Financial Company, Inc.
9730 SW Cascade Blvd., #200
Tigard, OR 97223-4324